Coaching Youth Tennis

FOURTH EDITION

American Sport Education Program

Official Handbook of USTA Jr. Team Tennis

Human Kinetics

Library of Congress Cataloging-in-Publication Data

American Sport Education Program.
Coaching youth tennis / American Sport Education Program. -- 4th ed.
p. cm.
"Official Handbook of USTA Jr. Team Tennis."
ISBN-13: 978-0-7360-6419-4 (soft cover)
ISBN-10: 0-7360-6419-2 (soft cover)
1. Tennis--Coaching. 2. Tennis for children--Coaching. I. United States Tennis Association. II. Title.
GV1002.9.C63A45 2008
796.34207'7--dc22
2008003276

ISBN-10: 0-7360-6419-2
ISBN-13: 978-0-7360-6419-4

Acquisitions Editor: Amy Tocco; **Project Writer:** Kirk Anderson; **Project Consultant:** Whitney Kraft; **Developmental Editor:** Laura Floch; **Assistant Editor:** Cory Weber; **Copyeditor:** Patsy Fortney; **Proofreader:** Julie Marx Goodreau; **Permission Manager:** Carly Breeding; **Graphic Designer:** Nancy Rasmus; **Graphic Artist:** Kim McFarland; **Cover Designer:** Keith Blomberg; **Photographer (cover):** © USTA; **Photographer (interior):** Frank Koester, unless otherwise noted; photos on pages 1, 9, 19, 33, 46, 49, 55, 67, 111, 127, 139 © Human Kinetics; **Photo Asset Manager:** Laura Fitch; **Visual Production Assistant:** Joyce Brumfield; **Photo Office Assistant:** Jason Allen; **Art Manager:** Kelly Hendren; **Associate Art Manager and Illustrator:** Alan L. Wilborn; **Printer:** United Graphics

We thank the USTA National Tennis Center in Queens, New York, for assistance in providing the location for the photo shoot for this book.

Copies of this book are available at special discounts for bulk purchase for sales promotions, premiums, fund-raising, or educational use. Special editions or book excerpts can also be created to specifications. For details, contact the Special Sales Manager at Human Kinetics.

Printed in the United States of America 10 9 8 7 6 5 4 3 2 1

Human Kinetics
Web site: www.HumanKinetics.com

United States: Human Kinetics
P.O. Box 5076
Champaign, IL 61825-5076
800-747-4457
e-mail: humank@hkusa.com

Canada: Human Kinetics
475 Devonshire Road Unit 100
Windsor, ON N8Y 2L5
800-465-7301 (in Canada only)
e-mail: info@hkcanada.com

Europe: Human Kinetics
107 Bradford Road
Stanningley
Leeds LS28 6AT, United Kingdom
+44 (0) 113 255 5665
e-mail: hk@hkeurope.com

Australia: Human Kinetics
57A Price Avenue
Lower Mitcham, South Australia 5062
08 8372 0999
e-mail: info@hkaustralia.com

New Zealand: Human Kinetics
Division of Sports Distributors NZ Ltd.
P.O. Box 300 226 Albany
North Shore City
Auckland
0064 9 448 1207
e-mail: info@humankinetics.co.nz

Contents

Welcome to Coaching v

Welcome From the United States Tennis Association vii

Activity Finder viii

Key to Diagrams xi

1 Stepping Into Coaching 1

2 Communicating as a Coach 9

3 Understanding Rules and Equipment 19

4 Providing for Players' Safety 33

5 Making Practices Fun and Practical 49

6 Teaching and Shaping Skills 55

7 Coaching Basic Tennis Skills 67

8 Coaching Singles and Doubles Play 111

9 Coaching on Match Day 127

10 Developing Season and Practice Plans 139

Appendix A: Related Checklists and Forms 153

Appendix B: Tennis Terms 159

Appendix C: 21 Tennis Activities 163

About ASEP and the USTA 175

Welcome to Coaching

Coaching young people is an exciting way to be involved in sport. But it isn't easy. Some coaches are overwhelmed by the responsibilities involved in helping athletes through their early sport experiences. And that's not surprising because coaching youngsters requires more than bringing the balls to the court and letting them play. It also involves preparing them physically and mentally to compete effectively, fairly, and safely in their sport and providing them with a positive role model.

This book will help you meet the challenges and experience the many rewards of coaching young athletes. You'll learn how to meet your responsibilities as a coach, communicate well and provide for safety, and teach skills while keeping them fun, and you'll learn strategies for coaching on match day. There are over 30 activities included throughout the text and in appendix C to help you with your practices. We also provide a sample practice plan and season plan to help guide you throughout your season.

This book serves as a text for ASEP's Coaching Youth Tennis course. If you would like more information about the American Sport Education Program or the United States Tennis Association, please contact us at the following addresses:

ASEP
P.O. Box 5076
Champaign, IL 61825-5076
800-747-5698
www.ASEP.com

USTA
70 West Red Oak Lane
White Plains, NY 10604
914-696-7000
www.USTA.com

Welcome From the United States Tennis Association

Dear Coach:

On behalf of the United States Tennis Association (USTA), welcome to *Coaching Youth Tennis*. This is one of many resources available to you through the American Sport Education Program (ASEP) and the United States Tennis Association. Whether you're learning how to teach proper fundamental skills or how to communicate better, this book can guide you through your experience of coaching young tennis players.

Here you will find fresh ideas on coaching children. Young players like to be with their friends and be part of a team, and this book will show you how to make tennis, a traditionally individual sport, an exciting team sport with practice sessions and team matches. The plans might be different from the way you were coached, but these methods are best for developing passionate players.

Written for coaches who do not have extensive experience, this book is full of ideas to help you through your first season and many more to come. You will find this complete introduction to coaching easy to follow and enjoyable to read.

Your coaching will have a profound and lasting impact on players you influence. Thank you for all you do for young athletes.

Sincerely,

Kirk Anderson
Director
Recreational Coaches and Programs

Scott Schultz
Managing Director
Recreational Tennis

Activity Finder

Skill	Activity	Page
Baseline		
Serve	Serving Drill	84
	Attack Serve and Take Net	165
	Beat Mr. Nobody	166
	Five Basic Returns	168
	Lob the Return	169
	Shadow Doubles	170
	Team Doubles	172
	The Deep Game	173
	Three-Shot Tennis	173
Forehand ground stroke	Forehand Ground Stroke Drill	87
	Alley Rally	164
	Crosscourt Rallies	168
	One Ball Live	170
	The Deep Game	173
	Three-Shot Tennis	173
Backhand ground stroke	Backhand Ground Stroke Drill	91
	Alley Rally	164
	Crosscourt Rallies	168
	One Ball Live	170
	The Deep Game	173
	Three-Shot Tennis	173
Lob	Lob Drill	93
	Baseline Doubles	165
	Lob the Giant	169
	Lob the Return	169
	Team Doubles	172
	Triples	174
Service return	Service Return Drill	96
	Five Basic Returns	168
	Lob the Return	169
	Shadow Doubles	170
	Team Doubles	172
	The Deep Game	173
	Three-Shot Tennis	173

Skill	Activity	Page
Midcourt		
Approach shot	Approach Shot Drill Attack Serve and Take Net Baseline Doubles	98 165 165
Drop shot	Drop Shot Drill	100
Sharp-angled crosscourt shot	Sharp-Angled Crosscourt Shot Drill	101
Net		
Volley	Volley Drill Circle Volley Shadow Doubles Stop Sign Volley Tap Team Doubles Triples Two Points at the Net	106 167 170 171 172 174 174
Overhead smash	Overhead Smash Drill Lob the Giant Two Points at the Net	110 169 174
Game play		
Doubles	All Position Doubles Baseline Doubles Champion of the Court Lob the Giant Lob the Return One Ball Live Shadow Doubles Team Doubles Triples Two Points at the Net	164 165 167 169 169 170 170 172 174 174
Singles	Champs and Chumps Champion of the Court Tag Team Singles Three-Shot Tennis	166 167 171 173

Key to Diagrams

- Player
- S Server
- SP Server's partner
- R Receiver
- RP Receiver's partner

1

Stepping Into Coaching

If you are like most youth league coaches, you have probably been recruited from the ranks of concerned parents, sport enthusiasts, or community volunteers. Like many rookie and veteran coaches, you probably have had little formal instruction on how to coach. But when the call went out for coaches to assist with the local youth tennis program, you answered because you like children and enjoy tennis, and perhaps because you wanted to be involved in a worthwhile community activity.

Your initial coaching assignment may be difficult. Like many volunteers, you may not know everything there is to know about tennis or about how to work with children. *Coaching Youth Tennis* presents the basics of coaching tennis effectively. To start, we look at your responsibilities and what's involved in being a coach. We also talk about what to do when your child is on the team you coach, and we examine five tools for being an effective coach.

Your Responsibilities as a Coach

Coaching at any level involves much more than establishing the lineup or teaching your players how to hit a spin serve. Coaching involves accepting the tremendous responsibility you face when parents put their children into your care. As a tennis coach, you'll be called upon to do the following:

1. *Provide a safe physical environment.*

   Playing tennis holds inherent risks. As a coach you're responsible for regularly inspecting the practice and competition courts and equipment (see the Facilities and Equipment Checklist in appendix A on page 154). Reassure players and parents that, to avoid injury, the players on your team will learn the safest techniques and that you have an emergency action plan (see chapter 4 for more information).

2. *Communicate in a positive way.*

   As you can already see, you have a lot to communicate. You'll communicate not only with your players and their parents but also with the coaching staff, administrators, and others. Communicate in a way that is positive and that demonstrates that you have the best interests of the players at heart (see chapter 2 for more information).

3. *Teach the fundamental skills of tennis.*

   When teaching the fundamental skills of tennis, keep in mind that tennis is a game, and as such, you want to be sure that your athletes have fun. Therefore, help all players be the best they can be by creating a fun, yet productive, practice environment. To help you do this, we'll show you an innovative games approach to teaching and practicing the skills young athletes need to know—an approach that kids thoroughly enjoy (see chapter 5 for more information). Additionally, to help your athletes improve their skills, you need to have a sound understanding of basic tennis skills and singles and doubles play (see chapters 7 and 8 for more information).

4. *Teach the rules of tennis.*

   Introduce the rules of tennis and incorporate them into individual instruction (see chapter 3 for more information). Many rules can be taught in practice, including calling lines, keeping score, the order of serving and receiving, playing a let, tiebreaks, changing sides, and touching the net during play. Plan to review the rules, however, any time an opportunity naturally arises during practice.

5. *Direct players in competition.*

   Directing players in competition includes determining starting lineups for both singles and doubles play, relating appropriately to opposing coaches and players, and making sound tactical decisions during matches (see chapter 9 for more information on coaching during matches). Remember that the focus is not on winning at all costs, but on coaching your kids to compete well, do their best, improve their tennis skills, and strive to win within the rules.

6. *Help your players become fit and value fitness for a lifetime.*

   Help your players be fit so they can play tennis safely and successfully. They should also learn to become fit on their own, understand the value of fitness, and enjoy training. Thus, do not make them do push-ups or run laps for punishment. Make it fun to get fit for tennis, and make it fun to play tennis so that they'll stay fit for a lifetime.

7. *Help young people develop character.*

   Good character traits to develop include enjoying learning, caring about others, being honest and respectful, and taking responsibility. These intangible qualities are no less important to teach than the skill of serving the ball. Encourage these traits in players by demonstrating and encouraging behaviors that express these traits at all times. For example, in doubles play, stress to young players the importance of learning their positions and responsibilities, communicating with their partners during points and supporting their partners after points, and showing respect for their opponents.

The preceding list outlines your responsibilities as a coach. Remember that every player is an individual, and provide a wholesome environment in which every player has the opportunity to learn how to play the game without fear while having fun and enjoying the overall tennis experience.

Coaching Your Own Child

Coaching can be complicated when your child plays on the team you coach. Many coaches are parents, but the two roles should not be confused. As a parent, you are responsible only for yourself and your child, but as a coach you are also responsible for the organization, all the players on the team, and their parents. Because of this additional responsibility, your behavior on the tennis court will be different from your behavior at home, and your son or daughter may not understand why.

Coaching Tip

It's important to discuss your interest in coaching the tennis team with your child before making a decision. If she has strong reservations about your taking over the head coach job, consider becoming involved in a smaller role instead, such as being an assistant coach, serving as the scorekeeper for the team, or organizing a group of parents who provide drinks and snacks at practices and matches.

For example, imagine the confusion of a young girl who is the center of her parents' attention at home but is barely noticed by her father (who is the coach) in the sport setting. Or consider the mixed signals a young boy receives when his mother, who rarely comments on his activities at home, evaluates him constantly as his coach. You need to explain to your child your new responsibilities and how they will affect your relationship when coaching. Take the following steps to avoid problems in coaching your own child:

- Ask your child if he wants you to coach the team.
- Explain why you want to be involved with the team.
- Discuss with your child how your interactions will change when you take on the role of coach at practices or matches.
- Limit your coaching behavior to when you are in the coaching role.
- Avoid parenting during practice or game situations to keep your role clear in your child's mind.
- Reaffirm your love for your child, irrespective of his performance on the tennis court.

Five Tools of an Effective Coach

Have you purchased the traditional coaching tools—things like whistles, coaching clothes, tennis shoes, a basket of balls, and a clipboard? They'll help you in the act of coaching, but to be successful, you'll need five other tools that cannot be bought. These tools are available only through self-examination and hard work; they're easy to remember with the acronym COACH:

C Comprehension

O Outlook

A Affection

C Character

H Humor

Comprehension

Comprehension of the rules and skills of tennis is required. You must understand the basic elements of the sport. To improve your comprehension of tennis, take the following steps:

- Read about the rules of tennis in chapter 3 of this book.
- Read about the fundamental skills of tennis in chapters 7 and 8.
- Read additional tennis coaching books, including those available from the American Sport Education Program (ASEP).
- Contact youth tennis organizations, such as the United States Tennis Association (USTA).
- Attend tennis coaching clinics and workshops.
- Talk with more experienced coaches.
- Observe local college, high school, and youth tennis matches.
- Watch tennis matches on television.

In addition to having tennis knowledge, you must implement proper training and safety methods so that your players can participate with little risk of injury. Even then, injuries may occur, and more often than not, you'll be the first person responding to them. Therefore, be sure you understand the basic emergency care procedures described in chapter 4. Also, read in that chapter how to handle more serious sport injury situations.

Coaching Tip

Local high school or college matches are a low-cost way not only to improve your knowledge of the game but also to allow players of any age to see the technical and tactical skills they're working on in action. Consider working with your team's parents to organize a team outing to a local match in place of an after-school or weekend practice.

Outlook

This coaching tool refers to your perspective and goals—what you seek as a coach. The most common coaching objectives are to (a) have fun; (b) help players develop their physical, mental, and social skills; and (c) strive to win.

Thus, your outlook includes your priorities, your planning, and your vision for the future. See Assessing Your Priorities to learn more about the priorities you set for yourself as a coach.

Assessing Your Priorities

Even though all coaches focus on competition, we want you to focus on positive competition—keeping the pursuit of victory in perspective by making decisions that, first, are in the best interest of the players and, second, will help to win the game.

So, how do you know whether your outlook and priorities are in order? Here's a little test:

1. Which situation would you be most proud of?
   a. *knowing that each participant enjoyed playing tennis*
   b. *seeing that all players improved their tennis skills*
   c. *winning the league championship*
2. Which statement best reflects your thoughts about sport?
   a. *if it isn't fun, don't do it.*
   b. *everyone should learn something every day.*
   c. *sport isn't fun if you don't win.*
3. How would you like your players to remember you?
   a. *as a coach who was fun to play for*
   b. *as a coach who provided a good base of fundamental skills*
   c. *as a coach who had a winning record*
4. Which would you most like to hear a parent of a player on your team say?
   a. *Max really had a good time playing tennis this year.*
   b. *Megan learned some important lessons playing tennis this year.*
   c. *Josh played on the first-place tennis team this year.*
5. Which of the following would be the most rewarding moment of your season?
   a. *having your team want to continue playing, even after practice is over*
   b. *seeing one of your players finally master the skill of hitting the overhead smash*
   c. *winning the championship*

Look over your answers. If you most often selected "a" responses, then having fun is most important to you. A majority of "b" answers suggests that skill development is what attracts you to coaching. And if "c" was your most frequent response, winning is tops on your list of coaching priorities. If your priorities are in order, your players' well-being will take precedence over your team's win-loss record every time.

ASEP has a motto that will help you keep your outlook in line with the best interests of the kids on your team. It summarizes in four words all you need to remember when establishing your coaching priorities:

Athletes First, Winning Second

This motto recognizes that striving to win is an important, even vital, part of sports. But it emphatically states that no efforts in striving to win should be made at the expense of the athletes' well-being, development, and enjoyment. Take the following actions to better define your outlook:

- With your coaches, determine your priorities for the season.
- Prepare for situations that challenge your priorities.
- Set goals for yourself and your players that are consistent with your priorities.
- Plan how you and your players can best attain your goals.
- Review your goals frequently to be sure that you are staying on track.

Affection

Another vital tool you will want to have in your coaching kit is a genuine concern for the young people you coach. This requires having a passion for kids, a desire to share with them your enjoyment and knowledge of tennis, and the patience and understanding that allow each player to grow from his or her involvement in sport. You can demonstrate your affection and patience in many ways, including the following:

- Make an effort to get to know each player on your team.
- Treat each player as an individual.
- Empathize with players trying to learn new and difficult skills.
- Treat players as you would like to be treated under similar circumstances.
- Control your emotions.
- Show your enthusiasm for being involved with your team.
- Keep an upbeat tempo and positive tone in all of your communications.

Character

The fact that you have decided to coach young tennis players probably means that you believe that participation in sport is important. But whether that participation develops character in your players depends as much on you as it does on the sport itself. In other words, to build character, you must exhibit it.

Having good character means modeling appropriate behaviors in sport and in life. That means more than just saying the right things. What you say and what you do must match. There is no place in coaching for the "Do as I say, not as I do" philosophy. Challenge, support, encourage, and reward every youngster, and your players will be more likely to accept, even celebrate, their differences. Be in control before, during, and after all practices and matches. And don't be afraid to admit that you were wrong. No one is perfect!

Each member of your coaching staff should consider the following steps to becoming a good role model:

- Take stock of your strengths and weaknesses.
- Build on your strengths.
- Set goals for yourself to improve in those areas you don't want to see copied.
- If you slip up, apologize to your team and to yourself. You'll do better next time.

Humor

Humor is an often-overlooked coaching tool. In this context it means having the ability to laugh at yourself and with your players during practices and matches. Nothing helps balance the seriousness of a skill session like a chuckle or two. And a sense of humor puts in perspective the many mistakes your players will make. So don't get upset over each miscue or respond negatively to erring players. Allow your players and yourself to enjoy the ups, and don't dwell on the downs. Here are some tips for injecting humor into your practices:

- Make practices fun by including a variety of activities.
- Keep all players involved in skill practices and activities.
- Consider your players' laughter as a sign of enjoyment, not of waning discipline.
- Smile!

Coaching Tip

Younger players in particular are often nervous about meeting new people and starting a new activity. A good way to break the ice with younger age groups is to tell a joke at the beginning of the first few practices. Here is an old standby:

Q: Why did it get really hot after the tennis match?

A: *All the fans went home!*

2

Communicating as a Coach

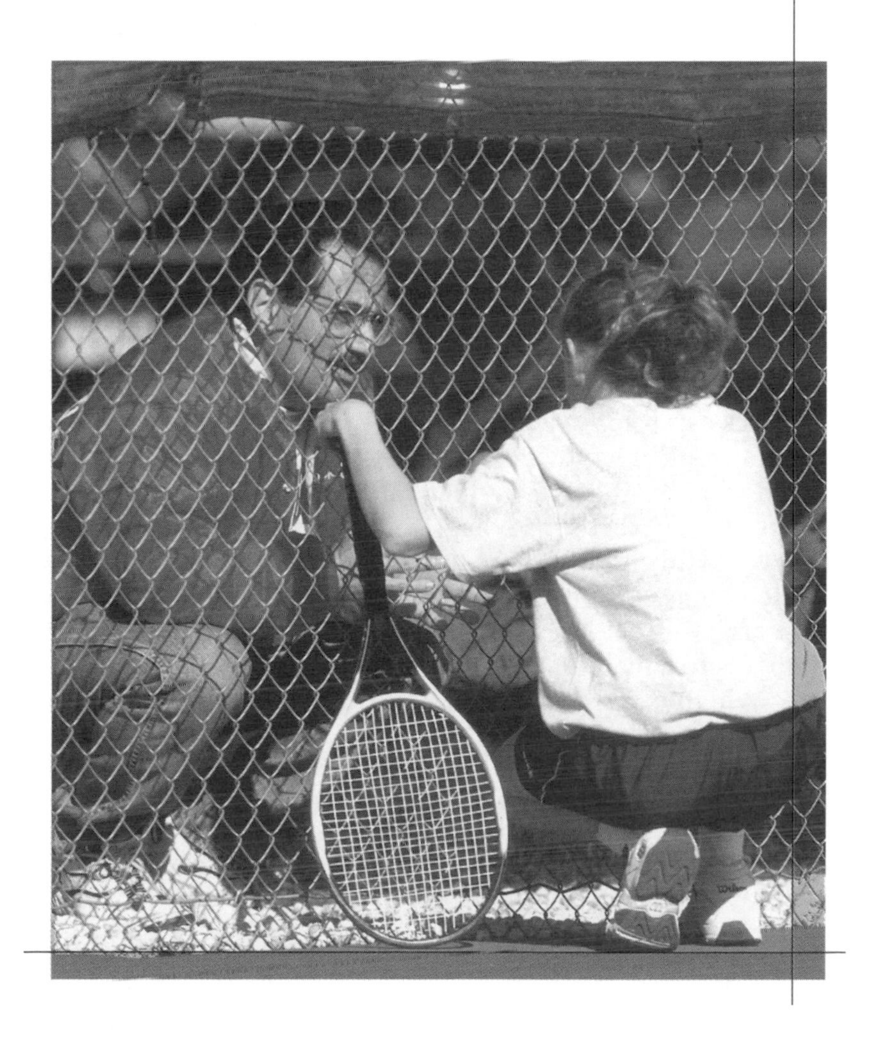

In chapter 1 you learned about the tools you need for coaching: comprehension, outlook, affection, character, and humor. These are essentials for effective coaching; without them, you'd have a difficult time getting started. But none of the tools will work if you don't know how to use them with your athletes—and this requires skillful communication. This chapter examines what communication is and how you can become a more effective communicator.

Coaches often mistakenly believe that communication occurs only when instructing players to do something, but verbal commands are only a small part of the communication process. More than half of what we communicate we do nonverbally. So remember when you are coaching: Actions speak louder than words.

Communication in its simplest form involves two people: a sender and a receiver. The sender transmits the message verbally, through facial expressions, and possibly through body language. Once the message is sent, the receiver must receive it and, optimally, understand it. A receiver who fails to pay attention or listen will miss part, if not all, of the message.

Sending Effective Messages

Young athletes often have little understanding of the rules and skills of tennis and probably even less confidence in their ability to play it. So they need accurate, understandable, and supportive messages to help them along. That's why your verbal and nonverbal messages are important.

Verbal Messages

"Sticks and stones may break my bones, but words will never hurt me" isn't true. Spoken words can have a strong and long-lasting effect. And coaches' words are particularly influential because youngsters place great importance on what coaches say. Perhaps you, like many former youth sport participants, have a difficult time remembering much of anything you were told by your elementary school teachers, but you can still recall several specific things your coaches at that level said to you. Such is the lasting effect of a coach's comments to a player.

Whether you are correcting misbehavior, teaching a player how to serve the ball, or praising a player for good effort, you should consider a number of things when sending a message verbally:

- Be positive and honest.
- State it clearly and simply.
- Say it loud enough, and say it again.
- Be consistent.

Be Positive and Honest

Nothing turns people off like hearing someone nag all the time, and athletes react similarly to a coach who gripes constantly. Kids particularly need encouragement because they often doubt their ability to perform in a sport. So look for and tell your players what they did well.

But don't cover up poor or incorrect play with rosy words of praise. Kids know all too well when they've erred, and no cheerfully expressed cliché can undo their mistakes. If you fail to acknowledge players' errors, your athletes will think you are a phony.

An effective way to correct a performance error is to first point out the part of the skill that the athlete performed correctly. Then explain—in a positive manner—the error the player made and show him the correct way to do it. Finish by encouraging the athlete and emphasizing the correct performance.

Be sure not to follow a positive statement with the word *but*. For example, you shouldn't say, "That was good work getting into position, Kelly. But if you bring your racket back sooner, you'll be able to keep the ball in the court." This causes many kids to ignore the positive statement and focus on the negative one. Instead, say, "That was good footwork preparation, Kelly. And if you bring your racket back sooner, you'll have more control of the ball. Way to go."

State It Clearly and Simply

Positive and honest messages are good, but only if expressed directly in words your players understand. Beating around the bush is ineffective and inefficient. And if you ramble, your players will miss the point of your message and probably lose interest. Here are tips for saying things clearly:

- Organize your thoughts before speaking to your athletes.
- Know your subject as completely as possible.
- Explain things thoroughly, but don't bore your athletes with long-winded monologues.
- Use language your players can understand, and be consistent in your terminology. However, avoid trying to be hip by using their age group's slang.

Say It Loud Enough, and Say It Again

Talk to your team in a voice that all members can hear. A crisp, vigorous voice commands attention and respect; garbled and weak speech is tuned out. It's okay and, in fact, appropriate to soften your voice when speaking to a player individually about a personal problem. But most of the time your messages will be for all your players to hear, so make sure they can! An enthusiastic voice also motivates players and tells them you enjoy being their coach. A word of caution, however: Avoid dominating the setting with a booming voice that distracts attention from players' performances.

Coaching Tip

Remember, terms that you are familiar with and understand may be completely foreign to your players, especially younger players and beginners. Adjust your vocabulary to match the age group. Although older players may understand terms such as *topspin lob* and *wrong foot your opponent,* beginners or younger players may be confused by this terminology. In some cases, you may need to use demonstrations so players can "see" the term and how it relates to the game of tennis.

Sometimes what you say, even if stated loudly and clearly, won't sink in the first time. This may be particularly true when young athletes hear words they don't understand. To avoid boring repetition and still get your message across, say the same thing in a slightly different way. For instance, you might first tell your players, "Follow through on your forehand!" If they don't appear to understand, you might say, "Bring your racket up and over your opposite shoulder after you hit the ball on your forehand side!" The second form of the message may get through to players who missed it the first time around.

Be Consistent

People often say things in ways that imply a different message. For example, a touch of sarcasm added to the words "Way to go!" sends an entirely different message than the words themselves suggest. Avoid sending mixed messages. Keep the tone of your voice consistent with the words you use. And don't say something one day and contradict it the next; players will get their wires crossed.

You also want to keep your terminology consistent. Many tennis terms describe the same or a similar skill. Take the side spin serve, for example. One coach may use the term *spin serve* to indicate a side spin serve, whereas another coach may say "kick it out wide." Although both are correct, to be consistent as a staff, agree on all terms before the start of the season and then stay with them.

Nonverbal Messages

Just as you should be consistent in the tone of voice and words you use, you should also keep your verbal and nonverbal messages consistent. An extreme example of failing to do this would be shaking your head, indicating disapproval, while at the same time telling a player "Nice try." Which is the player to believe, your gesture or your words?

Messages can be sent nonverbally in several ways. Facial expressions and body language are just two of the more obvious forms of nonverbal signals that can help you when you coach. Keep in mind that as a coach you need to be a teacher first; avoid any action that detracts from the message you are trying to convey.

Facial Expressions

The look on a person's face is the quickest clue to what she thinks or feels. Your players know this, so they will study your face, looking for a sign that will tell them more than the words you say. Don't try to fool them by putting on a happy or blank "mask." They'll see through it, and you'll lose credibility.

Serious, stone-faced expressions provide no cues to kids who want to know how they are performing. When faced with this, kids will just assume you're unhappy or disinterested. Don't be afraid to smile. A smile from a coach can give a great boost to an unsure athlete. Plus, a smile lets your players know that you are happy coaching them. But don't overdo it, or your players won't be able to tell when you are genuinely pleased by something they've done and when you are just putting on a smiling face.

Body Language

What might your players think if you come to practice slouched over, with your head down and shoulders slumped? They may think that you are tired, bored, or unhappy. What might they think if you watch them during a contest with a red face, your hands on your hips, and your jaw clenched? They may think that you are upset with them, disgusted at a line call, or mad at a fan. None of these is the impression you want your players to have of you. That's why you should carry yourself in a pleasant, confident, and vigorous manner.

Physical contact can also be a very important use of body language. A high-five, a pat on the head, an arm around the shoulder, and even a big hug are effective ways to show approval, concern, affection, and joy to your players. Youngsters are especially in need of this type of nonverbal message. Keep within the obvious moral and legal limits, of course, but don't be reluctant to touch your players, sending a message that can only be expressed in that way.

Coaching Tip

As a coach you should be aware of your body language. Because players of all ages will pick up on your actions and habits, provide a good example for your players to model. All it takes is a few eye rolls or wild hand gestures to send a message that this type of behavior is acceptable, even if that was never your intent.

Improving Receiving Skills

Now, let's examine the other half of the communication process: receiving messages. Too often very good message senders are very poor message receivers. As a coach of young athletes, you must be able to fulfill both roles effectively.

People seem to enjoy hearing themselves talk more than they do hearing others talk. For this reason, perhaps, receiving skills are often underdeveloped compared to sending skills. The requirements for receiving messages are quite simple, however. If you learn the keys to receiving messages and make a strong effort to use them with your players, you may be surprised by what you've been missing.

Pay Attention

First, you must pay attention; you must want to hear what others have to communicate to you. That's not always easy when you're busy coaching and have many things competing for your attention. But in one-on-one or team meetings with players, you must focus on what they are telling you, both verbally and nonverbally. You'll be amazed at the little signals you pick up. Not only will this focused attention help you catch every word your players say, but also you'll notice your players' moods and physical states. In addition, you'll get an idea of your players' feelings toward you and other players on the team.

Listen Carefully

How we receive messages from others, perhaps more than anything else we do, demonstrates how much we care for them and what they have to tell us. If you care little for your players or have little regard for what they have to say, it will show in how you listen to them. Check yourself. Do you find your mind wandering to what you are going to do after practice while one of your players is talking to you? Do you frequently have to ask your players, "What did you say?" If so, work on your receiving mechanics of attending and listening. However, if you're always missing the messages your players send, perhaps the most important question to ask yourself is "Do I want to be a coach?"

Providing Feedback

So far we've discussed separately the sending and receiving of messages. But we all know that senders and receivers switch roles several times during an interaction. One person initiates a communication by sending a message to another person, who then receives the message. The receiver then becomes the sender by responding to the person who sent the initial message. These verbal and nonverbal responses are called feedback.

Your players will look to you for feedback all the time. They will want to know how you think they are performing, what you think of their ideas, and whether their efforts please you. You can respond in many ways, and how you respond will strongly affect your players. They will react most favorably to positive feedback.

Praising players when they have performed or behaved well is an effective way of getting them to repeat (or try to repeat) that behavior. And positive feedback for effort is an especially effective way to motivate youngsters to work on difficult skills. So rather than shouting at and providing negative feedback to players who have made mistakes, try offering positive feedback and letting them know what they did correctly and how they can improve. Sometimes just the way you word feedback can make it more positive than negative. For example, instead of saying, "Don't hit the ball that way," you might say, "Hit the ball this way." Then your players will be focusing on what to do instead of what not to do.

Positive feedback can be verbal or nonverbal. Telling young players, especially in front of teammates, that they have performed well is a great way to boost their confidence. A pat on the back or a high-five also communicates that you recognize a player's performance.

Communicating With Others

Coaching involves not only sending and receiving messages and providing proper feedback to players but also interacting with members of the coaching staff, parents, fans, and opposing coaches. If you don't communicate effectively with these groups, your coaching career will be unpleasant and short lived. Try the following suggestions for communicating with these groups.

Coaching Staff

Before holding your first practice, arrange a meeting with your coaching staff to discuss the roles and responsibilities each coach will undertake during the year. Depending on the number of assistant coaches, the staff responsibilities can be divided into a number of areas. For example, one coach may be in charge of tactics and positioning while another is responsible for skill development. The head coach has the final responsibility for all phases of the game, but, as much as possible, the assistant coaches should be responsible for their areas.

Before practices start, the coaching staff should also discuss and agree on terminology, plans for practice, game-day organization, the method of communicating during practices and matches, and game conditions. The coaches on your staff must present a united front and speak with one voice, and they must all take a similar approach to coaching, interacting with the players and parents, and interacting with one another. Disagreements should be discussed away from the court where each coach can have a say and the staff can come to an agreement.

Parents

Players' parents need to be assured that their children are under the direction of a coach who is both knowledgeable about the sport and concerned about the youngsters' well-being. You can put their worries to rest by holding a preseason parent orientation meeting in which you describe your background and your approach to coaching. Although the type of paperwork needed before the season starts, the procedures for handing out equipment, and the costs of purchasing equipment will vary by team and league, the following

Preseason Meeting Topics offers a sample outline of information to cover at a parent orientation meeting.

Preseason Meeting Topics

1. Share your coaching philosophy.
2. Outline any paperwork that is needed:
   - Copy of player's birth certificate
   - Completed player application and payment record
   - Report card from previous year
   - Participation agreement form
   - Informed consent form
   - Emergency information card
3. Go over the inherent risks of tennis and other safety issues and review your emergency action plan.
4. Inform parents of necessary uniform and equipment requirements, including what items the league or team will provide and what players must furnish themselves.
5. Review the season practice schedule including the date, location, and time of each practice.
6. Go over proper attire for practices.
7. Discuss nutrition, hydration, and rest for players.
8. Explain the goals for the team.
9. Cover methods of communication: e-mail list, emergency phone numbers, interactive Web site, and so on.
10. Discuss ways that parents can help with the team.
11. Discuss standards of conduct for coaches, players, and parents.
12. Provide time for questions and answers.

If parents contact you with a concern during the season, listen to them closely and try to offer positive responses. If you need to communicate with parents, catch them after a practice or game, give them a phone call, or send a note through e-mail or regular mail. Messages sent to parents through players are too often lost, misinterpreted, or forgotten.

Fans

The stands probably won't be overflowing at your contests, which means that you'll more easily hear the few fans who criticize your coaching. When you hear something negative about the job you're doing, don't respond. Keep calm, consider whether the message had any value, and if not, forget it. Acknowledging critical, unwarranted comments from a fan during a contest will only encourage others to voice their opinions. So put away your "rabbit ears" and communicate to fans, through your actions, that you are a confident, competent coach.

Prepare your players, too, for fans' criticisms. Tell them it is you, not the spectators, they should listen to. If you notice that one of your players is rattled by a fan's comment, reassure the player that your evaluation is more objective and favorable—and the one that counts.

Opposing Coaches

Make an effort to visit with the coach of the opposing team before the match. During the match, don't get into a personal feud with the opposing coach. Remember, it's the kids, not the coaches, who are competing. By getting along well with the opposing coach, you'll show your players that competition involves cooperation.

3

Understanding Rules and Equipment

For youth tennis, USTA Jr. Team Tennis recommends that certain aspects of the competitive game be adjusted based on players' ages and skill levels to help them experience greater chances for success and enjoyment of the sport. Local leagues that follow USTA Jr. Team Tennis' recommendations retain young players because the players learn and compete on appropriate court sizes and use developmentally appropriate equipment. This chapter begins with a description of USTA Jr. Team Tennis to familiarize you with the organization.

Age Specifications for USTA Jr. Team Tennis

The QuickStart tennis format is based on six key specifications: age, court size, net height, racket length, ball type, and scoring. Note that this format is used only for players in the 10 and under and 8 and under age groups (players in the 12 and under age group and above play according to standard adult rules). The following table outlines the specifications for youth level play for the USTA Jr. Team Tennis age divisions of 8 and under, 10 and under, and 12 and under and above.

	Ages 8 and under	Ages 10 and under	Ages 12 and under and above
Type of play	QuickStart tennis format	QuickStart tennis format	Standard adult rules
Court size	36′ long and 18′ wide for both doubles and singles	60′ long and 21′ wide for singles and 27′ wide for doubles	78′ long and 27′ wide for singles and 36′ wide for doubles
Net height	2′9″	3′	3′6″ at the net post and 3′ at the center
Racket length	17″, 19″, 21″, or 23″	21″, 23″, or 25″	27″
Ball type	Foam or very low-compression standard-construction balls	Low-compression standard-construction balls	Standard-construction pressurized balls approved by USTA
Scoring	Best of three 7-point games	Two four-game sets, and if the match is tied after the two sets, a first-to-7-points set is used for a final set	Best of three six-game sets, and if the match is tied after two sets, a first-to-7-points set is used for a final set

USTA Jr. Team Tennis is a multiweek, coed youth tennis league that offers team practices and match play for girls and boys ages 6 to 18. Teams are composed of players of similar ages and skill levels, and they compete against other teams from the same geographic region in one of five age divisions: 8 and under, 10 and under, 12 and under, 14 and under, and 18 and under (this book covers only the four youngest divisions). Players in the 12 and under age group and above follow standard adult rules, but they are divided into three play levels (beginner, intermediate, and advanced) based on their NTRP (National Tennis Rating Program) rating (visit www.usta.com for more information). For the 8 and under and the 10 and under age groups, players are grouped solely based on age and participate using QuickStart tennis, a competitive format that allows young players to learn and play the game to scale based on age and skill level (for more information, see Age Specifications for USTA Jr. Team Tennis).

Court

The court on which a tennis match is played will vary depending on the age group of your players. As noted in Age Specifications for USTA Jr. Team Tennis, players in the 8 and under age group play on a 36 × 18 foot court, and players in the 10 and under age group play on a 60 × 21 foot court for singles and a 60 × 27 foot court for doubles. Players in the 12 and under age group and above play on a standard adult court that is 78 feet long and 27 feet wide for singles and 36 feet wide for doubles. See figure 3.1 for court dimensions for each of the three age groups.

In addition, the areas of the tennis court are referred to with special tennis terminology, as shown in figure 3.2. Here are a few definitions to help you better understand these areas:

- Forecourt—The area between the service line and the net.
- Backcourt—The area between the service line and the baseline.
- Singles court—A court on which singles tennis is played.
- Doubles court—A court on which doubles tennis is played.
- Service line—The line that runs parallel to the net from singles sideline to singles sideline. The service line marks the length of the service court, and serves must land on or inside the line to be good.
- Center service line—The line in the middle of the court that extends to the service line. The center service line marks the right side of the deuce court and the left side of the ad court. Serves must land on or inside the center service line to be good.
- Service court—The four courts within one full tennis court where serves are hit. Serves must be hit diagonally into the service court.

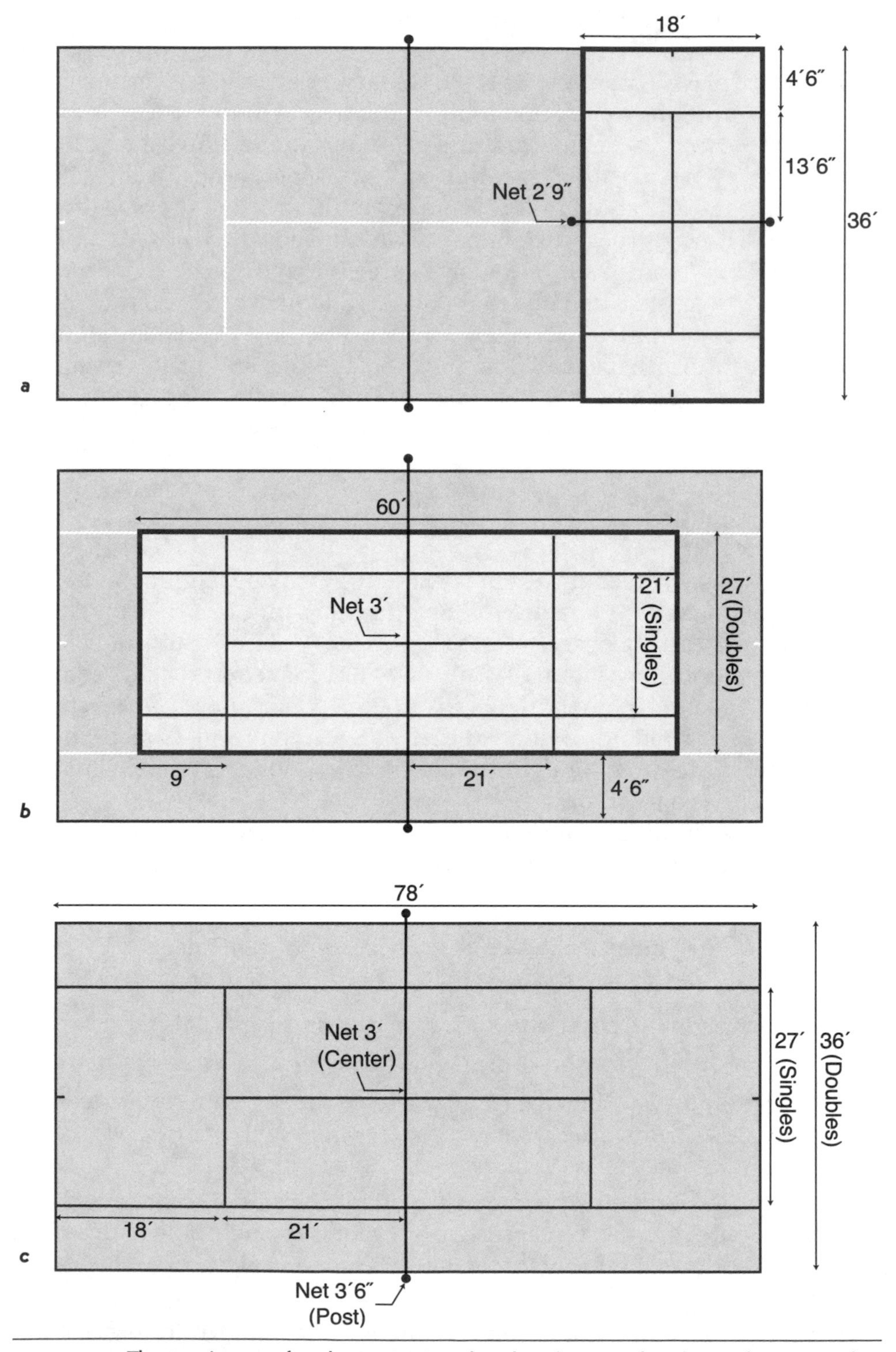

Figure 3.1 The tennis court for players *(a)* 8 and under, *(b)* 10 and under, and *(c)* 12 and under and above.

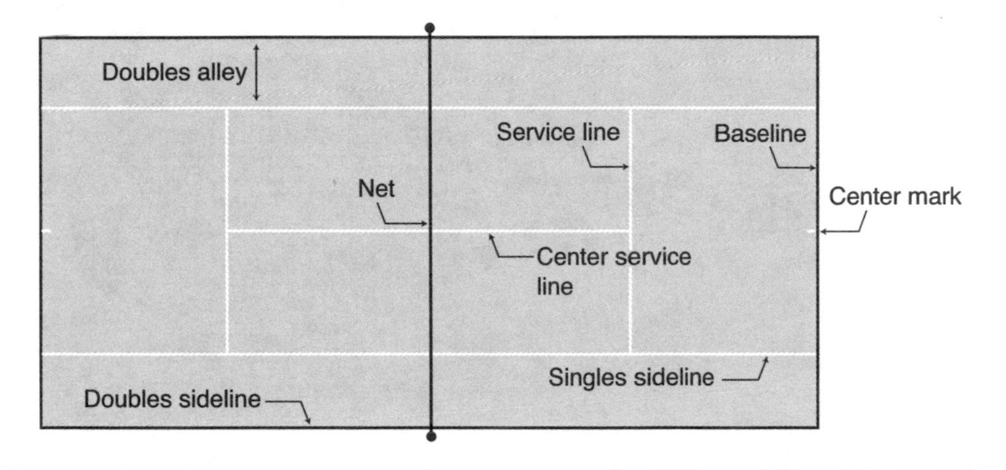

Figure 3.2 Tennis court areas.

- Center mark—The small line extending into the court located at the middle of the baseline that marks the right and left sides of the court for the server. The server must stand on the right side of the center mark when serving into the deuce court and on the left side of the center mark when serving into the ad court.
- Baseline—The line, parallel to the net, that marks the end of the court. Balls must land on or inside the baseline to be good during play for both singles and doubles.
- Singles sidelines—Lines that extend from baseline to baseline that mark the width of the court and also act as the outer lines of the service courts. Balls must land on or inside the singles sidelines when playing singles.
- Doubles sidelines—Lines that extend from baseline to baseline that are set wider than the singles sidelines to mark the width of the doubles court. Balls must land on or inside the doubles sidelines when playing doubles.

Equipment

The most standard pieces of equipment for tennis are rackets and balls. As a coach, you must examine the condition of each item your players use to be sure it meets acceptable standards. You should also make sure your players are outfitted properly. This section provides information on tennis equipment and apparel to help you keep your players well outfitted and equipped.

Rackets

A tennis racket, as shown in figure 3.3, is used to hit the ball back and forth over the net. Adult tennis rackets are made of strong, lightweight materials such as graphite or titanium; junior rackets are generally made of aluminum. The

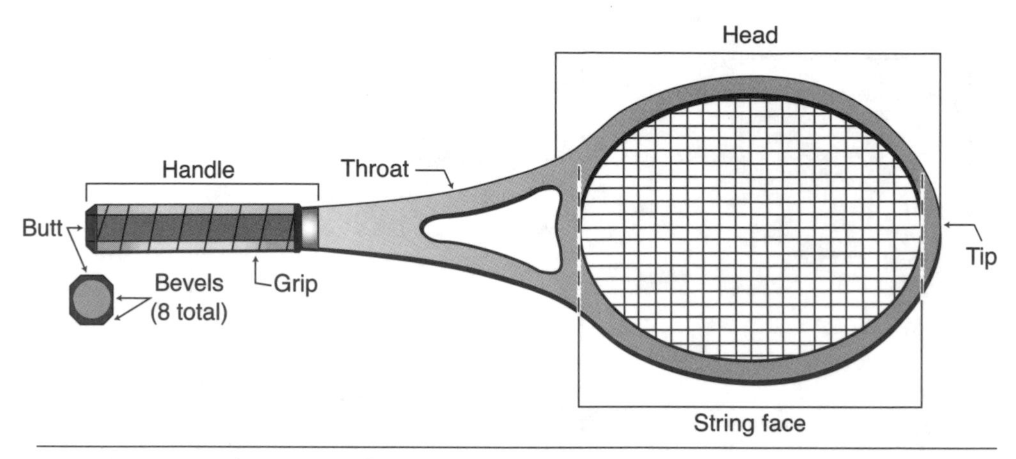

Figure 3.3 Parts of a tennis racket

face of a tennis racket is strung using a variety of materials including nylon, polyester, and Kevlar. The material used gives the string specific characteristics; some materials are more durable and hold up better for players hitting with heavy spins, whereas others provide more playability, comfort, and control.

The racket handle is wrapped with either a synthetic or a leather grip that can be tacky (so the hand won't slip) or dry (to absorb perspiration on hot days). The handle also has eight bevels—two are parallel with the racket face, two are perpendicular to the racket face, and four are at 45-degree angles to the racket face. These bevels prevent the hand from slipping when the ball is hit off-center and also provide reference points for the hand position on the handle for the variety of grips used during play.

A key factor in a player's success is the ability to control the racket. Younger or smaller children using a full-size 27-inch adult racket face three specific challenges: (a) the length of the racket is out of proportion to their arm length; (b) the weight is at the farthest point from the body when the arm is extended; and (c) smaller hands do not fit around the grip.

Young players need to use rackets whose lengths, weights, and grip sizes fit their smaller bodies and hands. Children ages 8 and under playing on a 36-foot court should use 17-, 19-, 21-, or 23- inch rackets, depending on their size. Children ages 10 and under playing on a 60-foot court should use 21-, 23-, or 25-inch rackets, again, depending on their size.

Coaching Tip

A racket should be the length from the ground to the end of the fingers when a child is standing straight with the arms down at the sides and the fingers pointing down.

Balls

The balls used for youth tennis differ depending on the age group you are working with. As noted in Age Specifications for USTA Jr. Team Tennis, players in the 8 and under age group use foam balls or very low-compression standard-construction balls, which are referred to as Stage 3 balls by the International

Tennis Federation (ITF). Stage 3 balls have red markings to distinguish them from other balls, and they are lighter, bounce lower, and move through the air at a slower speed. Foam balls are better suited for indoor play because they won't skid on a smooth surface, such as a wood or tile floor. Low-compression balls are better suited for outdoor play because they are slightly heavier and less affected by wind.

Players in the 10 and under age group use standard-construction low-compression balls, which are referred to as Stage 2 balls by the International Tennis Federation. Stage 2 balls have orange markings to distinguish them from other balls. These balls are heavier and move faster through the air than Stage 3 balls, but they are slower and bounce lower than standard balls (note that players in the 12 and under age group use standard-construction pressurized balls approved by the USTA).

Apparel

For matches, many schools, leagues, and clubs require players to wear uniforms that are alike in color and style. In most cases, this means that your players will wear matching shirts and shorts. For practices, however, instruct your players to wear attire that is both comfortable and safe. Most often, your players should wear T-shirts and shorts—basically, the type of clothing they'd wear to a match, but not their official uniform.

During both practices and games, players should wear clean tennis shoes and double-knot the laces to prevent them from coming untied, which can cause them to trip. Explain the importance of wearing shoes designed for court play because they provide the lateral stability needed for tennis. Players should not wear running shoes or sandals for either practices or matches.

Coaching Tip

Teach players to dress in layers for practices and competitions when the weather is cool so they can remove outer layers as they warm up. Warm-up suits with jackets and pants are ideal because they are easy to take off and put back on as players warm up or cool down, and many even have pockets that can be used for extra balls. Just remember that all clothing should be loose enough to allow for a full range of motion.

Players are not required to wear hats or visors during games, but many wear them to protect themselves from the sun, to shield their eyes from the sun, and to keep their hair from falling over their eyes. Additionally, players with long hair should pull their hair back off their faces with headbands or ponytail holders. Although there are no specific rules about jewelry, for safety reasons, it should be avoided if it is a distraction during play.

Rules of Play

Tennis is played worldwide in accordance with the official rules established by the International Tennis Federation. For both singles and doubles play, USTA Jr. Team Tennis adheres to those rules as well as *The Code*, which consists of "unwritten" rules of tennis that custom and tradition dictate players follow in matches (see Following *The Code*). The following sections outline the rules for scoring, serving, starting play, playing a point, and calling lines.

Following *The Code*

As mentioned previously, tennis has "unwritten" rules—called *The Code*—that custom and tradition dictate players follow. Tennis is unique in that most competitive matches are self-officiated, meaning that the players are responsible for keeping track of the score and making line calls (determining whether the ball is good or outside the line). Here are some basic guidelines, based on *The Code*, that you should teach your young tennis players:

- When standing near a tennis court in use, players must be silent or talk quietly so that they do not disturb those who are playing.
- Players should never walk behind a court in use until those playing have finished their point, so that they are not distracted.
- When your players are ready to play, they should move all extra equipment (racket covers, ball cans, bags, clothing, etc.) off the court and out of the way.
- Players should introduce themselves to their opponents before beginning the on-court warm-up. Note that the on-court warm-up is a short amount of time, usually about 5 minutes, that players are allowed once their game has been called. This on-court warm-up differs from the team warm-up that is discussed in chapter 9.
- Players must keep the game moving. Attempts to stall or to extend rest periods are illegal.
- Intentional distractions that interfere with an opponent's concentration or effort to play the ball are against the rules.
- If a serve is out, players should not return it. It is recommended that players tap the ball gently into the net or let it go behind them.
- If a ball goes into another court where players are playing, the players should wait until the other players finish their point before asking for the ball. If a ball from an adjacent court comes onto your players' court, they should return it as soon as play has stopped on both courts.
- Players are responsible for all line calls (for more information, see Calling Lines on page 31) and must accept all calls made by the opponent on his side of the court.
- The server is responsible for announcing the score before each point is played. The server should call it loud enough so the receiver can hear and should be sure the receiver is ready before serving the next point.
- If there is any disagreement on the score, players can return to the last score that they agree on and play from that score.

- After the last point, players should approach the net immediately and shake hands with their opponents, letting the opponents know that they appreciated the match, no matter the outcome.

Scoring

Traditionally, players of all ages and ability levels, including youth players, used the scoring system that adult tennis players used. USTA Jr. Team Tennis' QuickStart format provides a developmentally appropriate scoring system for each age group. By taking into account children's physical and mental development, these scoring systems ensure that young players understand the scoring format and enjoy playing the game.

Tennis competition is broken down as follows:

- Points make up games.
- Games make up sets.
- Sets make up the match.

Following are the basic scoring formats for each of the youth age groups.

8 and Under

To win tennis matches, players in the 8 and under age group must win two out of three 7-point games. Players in this age group don't play sets; this shortens and simplifies matches, making them more appropriate for younger players. For each game, each player serves for 2 points and score is kept numerically until one player totals 7 points. As soon as the first game is complete, a second game to 7 points follows. If the winner of the first game wins the second game, the match is complete. If each player has won one of the first two 7-point games, a third 7-point game is played as the deciding game, and the winner of that game wins the match. Matches generally take 10 to 20 minutes to complete.

10 and Under

Tennis matches for the 10 and under age group last longer than those for the 8 and under age group, but they are shorter than adult matches. To win a set, players in the 10 and under age group must win four games rather than six. The first player to win two sets wins the match. If each player has won a set, the match is determined by a tiebreak in which the first player or team to win 7 points wins the match.

12 and Under and Above

Players 12 and under and all older age groups play according to standard adult rules in which the first to win two six-game sets is the winner of the match. A player must be ahead by at least two games to win the set. If both players have won six games (i.e., neither is ahead by two games), they play a tiebreak in which the first player to win 7 points (by a margin of 2) wins the set.

Games consist of four points that are named 15, 30, 40, and game point. Zero is called "love." In each game, the first player to win a point has a score of 15, and the other player has no points, or love. The server's score is always announced first, so if the server wins the first point, the score is announced as 15-love. If the server wins the next point, the score is 30-love. If the server wins the third point, the score is 40-love, and if the server wins the fourth point, this is considered *game*, or the end of the game, because the player has won by at least two points. Now, let's assume the receiver has won points in the game. If the receiver wins the first point, the score is love-15. If the server wins the second point, the score is 15-all, indicating that the players are tied. If the receiver has two points and the server has one, the score is 15-30. If the receiver has three points and the server has one, it is 15-40.

If both players have three points, the score is 40-40, which is called deuce. The player who wins the point after deuce has what is called the advantage, which is referred to as "ad-in" for the server and "ad-out" for the receiver. The first player to win two points in a row after deuce wins the game. If one player wins a point and the other player then wins a point, the score goes back to deuce.

If the score is five games all, a player has to win the next two games to win the set seven to five. At six games all, players play a tiebreak and the player who wins tiebreak wins the set. When that happens, the score is recorded as seven to six. The first player to win two sets in the best of three sets wins the match.

For the tiebreak, the first player (or doubles team) to win 7 points wins the game and the set provided he leads by a margin of 2 points. If the score reaches 6 points all, the game is extended until this margin has been achieved. Numerical scoring (1, 2, 3, etc.) is used throughout the tiebreak game. The player whose turn it is to serve is the server for the first point; the opponent is the server for the second and third points; and thereafter, each player serves alternately for 2 consecutive points until the winner of the tiebreak has been decided.

Serving

For the first point, the server puts the ball in play by serving from behind the baseline and between the sideline and center mark, without stepping on or over the baseline before hitting the ball. Serves are delivered alternately from the right and left courts, beginning from the right, meaning that the first server serves the first point from the right court, the second server serves the second point from the left court, the third server serves the third point from the right court, and so on.

Starting Play

To begin play, your players must determine several things. First, to begin a match, before the first game, your player (or one of your players for doubles) will spin a racket or toss a coin. Any player can make the spin or toss, and the other player makes the call. The player that wins the coin toss or spin may choose one of the following three options:

1. Choose to serve or receive first
2. Choose which end of the court to begin playing on
3. Give your opponent the choice of deciding either whether to serve or receive or which end of the court to start at

Note that for doubles, either player on the team serving first may begin the match. Either person on the opposing team may receive the first ball in the right (or deuce) court. Also, for doubles, the receiving team may choose which player will play which court; however, they must then keep the order of serving and the sides for receiving for the whole set.

After the first game, players change ends of the court, and the receiver becomes the server for the next game. The player who served the previous game will receive serve throughout the next game. Players should switch ends again after the third, fifth, and every following odd-numbered game.

In a tiebreak, players change ends after every 6 points and at the conclusion of the tiebreak. The player (or doubles team) who served first in the tiebreak should receive serve in the first game of the following set.

Each serve must be hit diagonally over the net and into the receiver's service court, landing inside or on the lines of the service court. For example, if the server is serving from the right service court, the serve must land inside the opponent's right service court.

Your players must understand the meaning of deuce and ad court, especially when serving. When the server is serving from the right side of the center mark, he hits the ball diagonally into the opponent's right service court, which is called the deuce court. All games and even-numbered points begin with a serve to the deuce court. When the server is serving from the left side of the center mark, he hits the ball diagonally into the opponent's left service court, which is called the ad court. All odd-numbered points begin with a serve to this court.

A player makes a call when the ball is hit to her side of the court. Calls should be made as soon as the ball lands on the court and loud enough so the opponent can hear the call. Following are the three calls players are expected to make:

- *Out or good.* If a ball is hit after the serve is in play and does not land on or inside the singles or doubles court, it is considered out. If the ball lands in the court or on the line, it is considered good.
- *Fault.* If the first serve doesn't land in the correct court, it is called a fault and the player gets a second serve to put the ball in play to begin the point. If the server fails to hit the ball into the correct court on the second serve, it is called a double fault and the opponent wins that point. In doubles, if the server's partner is hit with the serve, a fault is called, but if the receiver's partner is hit with the serve before it touches the court, the server wins the point.
- *Let.* If the server hits a ball that touches the top of the net and lands into the correct service court, it is called a let. The server gets to take that serve again. If the server hits a ball that touches the top of the net and lands outside the correct service court, it is a fault. A serve that hits the net post or any other permanent fixture (such as a bench, light post, or fence) is also a fault.

Playing a Point

As learned previously, the serve is used to start a point, and the position of the server and where the ball must land are well defined in the rules of tennis. After the serve lands in the correct court, however, the point begins and players may position themselves anywhere—in or out of the court—on their own sides of the net.

Players also have the choice of hitting the ball before it bounces or after one bounce, but the receiver must let the serve bounce once before hitting it. In addition, the ball is still in play if it happens to touch the net or post. Players should continue the point when a ball lands on a boundary line of the court.

A player wins the point if she hits the ball over the net, it lands on or inside the lines of the court, and the opponent doesn't return it. A player loses the point if she hits the ball into the net or out of the court (unless the opponent touches the outgoing ball, meaning that it hits anything that she is carrying or wearing). A player also loses the point if the ball touches her clothing, if her racket touches the net or post, if she hits the ball before it passes the net, or if she deliberately hits the ball more than once. Players are on their honor to make these calls against themselves.

Calling Lines

As mentioned briefly in Following *The Code*, tennis is unique in that for the majority of matches, officiating is handled by the players. Your players are responsible for knowing and following the rules of the game, keeping track of and announcing the score, determining whether balls are playable, and handling any disputes that might arise on the court. Even so, it may be helpful to have an experienced player help with the line calling and scorekeeping for younger age groups. These volunteer officials should stand at the net post and assist with calls and announce the score before each point is played.

Teach your players the following guidelines to help them make proper line calls:

- If the ball lands on or inside the line and you cannot return it, it is considered good. Extend your hand with your palm facing the court, as shown in figure 3.4*a*, designating to your opponent that the ball was good.
- Call the ball out only when you can clearly see a space between where the ball lands on the court and the line. If you cannot see whether a ball is definitely out, continue playing the point.
- Make out calls immediately and audibly, and use a hand signal, as shown in figure 3.4*b*, with the index finger pointing up. Even if your opponent does not hear the out call, he will be able to see the signal.
- A call cannot be changed and a point stands as played, even if a ball mark found after the point indicates that the shot was out.

a

b

Figure 3.4 Hand signals: *(a)* good and *(b)* out.

- If you fail to see whether a ball that goes past you is in or out, you must award the point to your opponent.
- If you catch the ball before it bounces, even if you think it might land out and even if you are standing outside of the court, you lose the point.

4

Providing for Players' Safety

One of your players dives to return a solid backhand down the line. She hits the ball, but falls to the ground. You notice that she is not getting up from the ground and seems to be in pain. What do you do?

No coach wants to see players get hurt, but injury remains a reality of sport participation. Consequently, you must be prepared to provide first aid when injuries occur and to protect yourself against unjustified lawsuits. Fortunately, coaches can institute many preventive measures to reduce the risk. In this chapter we describe steps you can take to prevent injuries, first aid and emergency responses for when injuries occur, and your legal responsibilities as a coach.

Game Plan for Safety

You can't prevent all injuries from happening, but you can take preventive measures that give your players the best chance for injury-free participation. We'll explore what you can do in the following areas to create the safest possible environment for your athletes:

- Preseason physical examinations
- Physical conditioning
- Facilities and equipment inspection
- Player match-ups and inherent risks
- Proper supervision and record keeping
- Environmental conditions

Preseason Physical Examinations

We recommend that your players have physical examinations before participating in tennis. The exam should address the most likely areas of medical concern and identify youngsters at high risk. We also suggest that you have players' parents or guardians sign a participation agreement form (this will be discussed in more detail later in this chapter) and an informed consent form to allow their children to be treated in case of an emergency. For a sample form, see the Informed Consent Form in appendix A on page 155.

Physical Conditioning

Players need to be in shape or get in shape to play the game at the level expected. They must have adequate cardiorespiratory fitness and muscular fitness.

Cardiorespiratory fitness involves the body's ability to use oxygen and fuels efficiently to power muscle contractions. As players get in better shape, their bodies are able to more efficiently deliver oxygen to fuel muscles and carry off carbon dioxides and other wastes. At times, tennis will require lots of running and exertion. Youngsters who aren't as fit as their peers often overextend in trying to keep up, which can result in lightheadedness, nausea, fatigue, and sometimes injury.

Remember that the players' goals are to participate, learn, and have fun. If you keep them active, attentive, and involved during every phase of practice, they will attain higher levels of cardiorespiratory fitness as the season progresses simply by taking part in practice. However, watch closely for signs of low cardiorespiratory fitness; don't let your athletes do too much until they're fit. You might privately suggest to youngsters who appear overly winded that they train under proper supervision outside of practice to increase their fitness.

Coaching Tip
Because younger players may not know when they need a break for water and a short rest, work breaks into your practice schedules. In addition, have water available at all times during the practice session. Players have different hydration needs, and this will allow them to grab a drink when they need it, with the added benefit of reducing the need for long water breaks.

Muscular fitness encompasses strength, muscular endurance, power, speed, and flexibility. This type of fitness is affected by physical maturity, as well as strength training and other types of training. Your players will likely exhibit a relatively wide range of muscular fitness. Those who have greater muscular fitness will be able to run faster and hit harder than those who do not. They will also sustain fewer muscular injuries, and any injuries that do occur will tend to be minor. In case of injury, recovery is faster in those with higher levels of muscular fitness.

Two other components of fitness and injury prevention are the warm-up and the cool-down. Although young bodies are generally very limber, they too can become tight through inactivity. The warm-up should address each muscle group and elevate the heart rate in preparation for strenuous activity. Players should warm up for 5 to 10 minutes using a combination of light running, jumping, and stretching. As practice winds down, slow players' heart rates with an easy jog or walk. Then have players stretch for five minutes to help prevent tight muscles before the next practice or match.

Facilities and Equipment Inspection

Another way to prevent injuries is to examine regularly the court on which your players practice and play. Remove hazards, report conditions you cannot remedy (be aware that even damp courts are slippery and should not be used), and request maintenance as necessary. If unsafe conditions exist, either make adaptations to prevent risk to your players' safety or stop the practice or match until safe conditions have been restored. You can also prevent injuries by checking the quality and fit of shoes, uniforms, practice attire, and any protective equipment your players use. The Facilities and Equipment Checklist on page 154 in appendix A will help guide you in verifying that facilities and equipment are safe.

Player Match-Ups and Inherent Risks

We recommend that you group teams in two-year age increments if possible. You'll encounter fewer mismatches in physical maturation with narrow age ranges. Even so, two 12-year-old girls might differ by 60 pounds in weight, a foot in height, and three or four years in emotional and intellectual maturity. This presents dangers for the less mature player. Whenever possible, match players against opponents of similar size and physical maturity. Such an approach gives smaller, less mature youngsters a better chance to succeed and avoid injury while providing more mature players with a greater challenge. Supervise practices and matches closely to ensure that the more mature players do not put the less mature players at undue risk.

> **Coaching Tip**
> If your players vary largely in size, have players of similar size hit to each other during the warm-up. This will help prevent bigger players from hitting the ball too hard to smaller, less mature players who may have trouble handling hard hits.

Although proper matching helps protect you from certain forms of liability, you must also warn players of the inherent risks involved in playing tennis. "Failure to warn" is one of the most successful arguments in lawsuits against coaches. So, thoroughly explain the inherent risks of tennis, and make sure each player knows, understands, and appreciates those risks. Learn more about inherent risks by talking with your league administrators.

The preseason parent orientation meeting is a good opportunity to explain the risks of the sport to both parents and players. It is also a good time to have both the players and their parents sign a participation agreement form or waiver releasing you from liability should an injury occur. Work with your league when creating these forms or waivers, and have legal counsel review them prior to presenting them to players and their parents. Although these forms or waivers do not relieve you of responsibility for your players' well-being, they are recommended by lawyers and may help you in the event of a lawsuit.

Proper Supervision and Record Keeping

To ensure players' safety, you must provide both general and specific supervision. General supervision means that you are in the area of activity so that you can see and hear what is happening. You should be

- on the court and in position to supervise the players even before the formal practice begins,
- immediately accessible to the activity and able to oversee the entire activity,
- alert to conditions that may be dangerous to players and ready to take action to protect players,

- able to react immediately and appropriately to emergencies, and
- present on the court until the last player has been picked up after the practice or match.

Specific supervision is the direct supervision of an activity at practice. For example, you should provide specific supervision when you teach new skills and continue it until your athletes understand the requirements of the activity, the risks involved, and their own ability to perform in light of these risks. You must also provide specific supervision when you notice either players breaking rules or a change in the condition of your athletes. As a general rule, the more dangerous the activity, the more specific the supervision required. This suggests that more specific supervision is required with younger and less experienced athletes.

Coaching Tip

Common sense tells us that it's easier to provide specific supervision to a smaller group of players, regardless of age. Enlist the help of assistant coaches to divide your team into smaller groups to ensure that players can practice skills in a safe environment. The more adults who can help supervise, the better the players can learn and perform the skills of tennis. In addition, smaller groups allow coaches to provide more direct feedback to players.

As part of your supervision duty, you are expected to foresee potentially dangerous situations and to be positioned to help prevent them. This requires that you know tennis well, especially the rules that are intended to provide for safety. Prohibit dangerous horseplay, and hold training sessions only under safe weather conditions. These specific supervisory activities, applied consistently, will make the play environment safe for your players and will help protect you from liability if a mishap occurs.

For further protection, keep records of your season plans, practice plans, and players' injuries. Season and practice plans come in handy when you need evidence that players have been taught certain skills, whereas accurate, detailed injury report forms offer protection against unfounded lawsuits. Ask for these forms from your sponsoring organization (see page 156 in appendix A for a sample injury report form), and hold onto these records for several years so that an "old tennis injury" of a former player doesn't come back to haunt you.

Environmental Conditions

Most health problems caused by environmental factors are related to excessive heat or cold, although you should also consider other factors such as severe weather and air pollution. A little thought about the potential problems and a little effort to ensure adequate protection for your athletes will prevent most serious emergencies related to environmental conditions.

Heat

On hot, humid days the body has difficulty cooling itself. Because the air is already saturated with water vapor (humidity), sweat doesn't evaporate as easily. Therefore, body sweat is a less effective cooling agent, and the body retains extra heat. Hot, humid environments put athletes at risk of heat exhaustion and heatstroke (see more on these under Serious Injuries on pages 45-47). And if *you* think it's hot or humid, it's worse for the kids, not only because they're more active, but also because kids under the age of 12 have more difficulty regulating their body temperature than adults do. To provide for players' safety in hot or humid conditions, take the following preventive measures:

- Monitor weather conditions and adjust training sessions accordingly. Table 4.1 shows the specific air temperatures and humidity percentages that can be hazardous.
- Acclimatize players to exercising in high heat and humidity. Athletes can adjust to high heat and humidity in 7 to 10 days. During this period, hold practices at low to moderate activity levels and give the players fluid breaks every 20 minutes.
- Switch to light clothing. Players should wear shorts and white T-shirts.
- Identify and monitor players who are prone to heat illness. Players who are overweight, heavily muscled, or out of shape or players who work excessively hard or have suffered previous heat illness are more prone to heat illness. Monitor these athletes closely and give them fluid breaks every 15 to 20 minutes.
- Make sure athletes replace fluids lost through sweat. Encourage players to drink 17 to 20 ounces of fluid two to three hours before practice or matches and 7 to 10 ounces every 20 minutes during practice and after practice. Afterward they should drink 16 to 24 ounces of fluid for every pound lost during exercise. Fluids such as water and sports drinks are preferable during matches and practices (suggested intakes are based on NATA [National Athletic Trainers' Association] recommendations).
- Replenish electrolytes, such as sodium (salt) and potassium, that are lost through sweat. The best way to replace these nutrients in addition to others such as carbohydrate (energy) and protein (muscle building) is by eating a balanced diet. Experts say that during the most intense training periods in the heat, additional salt intake may be helpful.

Coaching Tip

Encourage players to drink plenty of water before, during, and after practice. Water makes up 45 to 65 percent of a youngster's body weight, and even a small amount of water loss can cause severe consequences in the body's systems. It doesn't have to be hot and humid for players to become dehydrated, nor is thirst an accurate indicator of dehydration. In fact, by the time players are aware of their thirst, they are long overdue for a drink.

Table 4.1 Warm-Weather Precautions

Temperature (°F)	Humidity	Precautions
80-90	<70%	Monitor athletes prone to heat illness
80-90	>70%	5-minute rest after 30 minutes of practice
90-100	<70%	5-minute rest after 30 minutes of practice
90-100	>70%	Short practices in evening or early morning

Cold

When a person is exposed to cold weather, body temperature starts to drop below normal. To counteract this reaction, the body shivers to create heat and reduces blood flow to the extremities to conserve heat in the core of the body. But no matter how effective its natural heating mechanism is, the body will better withstand cold temperatures if it is prepared to handle them. To reduce the risk of cold-related illnesses, make sure players wear appropriate protective clothing and keep them active to maintain body heat. Also monitor the windchill factor, because it can drastically affect the severity of players' responses to the weather. The windchill factor index is shown in figure 4.1.

Temperature (°F)

Wind speed (mph)	0	5	10	15	20	25	30	35	40
40	-55	-45	-35	-30	-20	-15	-5	0	10
35	-50	-40	-35	-30	-20	-10	-5	5	10
30	-50	-40	-30	-25	-20	-10	0	5	10
25	-45	-35	-30	-20	-15	-5	0	10	15
20	-35	-30	-25	-15	-10	0	5	10	20
15	-30	-25	-20	-10	-5	0	10	15	25
10	-20	-15	-10	0	5	10	15	20	30
5	-5	0	5	10	15	20	25	30	35

Flesh may freeze within one minute (shaded cells)

Windchill temperature (°F)

Figure 4.1 Windchill factor index.

Severe Weather

Severe weather refers to a host of potential dangers, including lightning storms, tornadoes, hail, and heavy rain. Lightning is of special concern because it can come up quickly and can cause great harm or even kill. For each 5-second count from the flash of lightning to the bang of thunder, lightning is one mile away. A flash-bang of 10 seconds means lightning is two miles away;

a flash-bang of 15 seconds means lightning is three miles away. A practice or competition should be stopped for the day if lightning is six miles away or closer (30 seconds or less from flash to bang). In addition to these suggestions, your school, league, or state association may have additional rules regarding severe weather that you should consider.

Safe places in which to take cover when lightning strikes are fully enclosed metal vehicles with the windows up, enclosed buildings, and low ground (under cover of bushes, if possible). It's not safe to be near metal objects such as flagpoles, fences, light poles, and metal bleachers. Also avoid trees, water, and open fields.

Cancel practice when under either a tornado watch or a tornado warning. If you are practicing or competing when a tornado is nearby, you should get inside a building if possible. If you cannot get into a building, lie in a ditch or other low-lying area or crouch near a strong building, and use your arms to protect your head and neck.

The keys to handling severe weather are caution and prudence. Don't try to get that last 10 minutes of practice in if lightning is on the horizon. And don't continue to play in rain, even if it is a light rain. Respect the weather and play it safe.

Air Pollution

Poor air quality and smog can present real dangers to your players. Both short- and long-term lung damage are possible from participating in unsafe air. Although it's true that participating in clean air is not possible in many areas, restricting activity is recommended when the air-quality ratings are lower than moderate or when there is a smog alert. Your local health department or air-quality control board can inform you of the air-quality ratings for your area and when restricting activities is recommended.

Responding to Players' Injuries

No matter how good and thorough your prevention program is, injuries most likely will occur. When injury does strike, chances are you will be the one in charge. The severity and nature of the injury will determine how actively involved you'll be in treating it. But regardless of how seriously a player is hurt, it is your responsibility to know what steps to take. Therefore, you must be prepared to take appropriate action and provide basic emergency care when an injury occurs.

Being Prepared

Being prepared to provide basic emergency care involves many things, including being trained in cardiopulmonary resuscitation (CPR) and first aid and having an emergency action plan.

CPR and First Aid Training

We recommend that all coaches receive CPR and first aid training from a nationally recognized organization such as the National Safety Council, the American Heart Association, the American Red Cross, or the American Sport Education Program (ASEP). You should be certified based on a practical test and a written test of knowledge. CPR training should include pediatric and adult basic life support and obstructed airway procedures.

First Aid Kit

A well-stocked first aid kit should include the following:

- Antibacterial soap or wipes
- Arm sling
- Athletic tape—1 1/2 inches wide
- Bandage scissors
- Bandage strips—assorted sizes
- Blood spill kit
- Cell phone
- Contact lens case
- Cotton swabs
- Elastic wraps—3 inches, 4 inches, and 6 inches
- Emergency blanket
- Examination gloves—latex free
- Eye patch
- Foam rubber—1/8 inch, 1/4 inch, and 1/2 inch
- Insect sting kit
- List of emergency phone numbers
- Mirror
- Moleskin
- Nail clippers
- Oral thermometer (to determine whether an athlete has a fever caused by illness)
- Penlight
- Petroleum jelly
- Plastic bags for crushed ice
- Prewrap (underwrap for tape)
- Rescue breathing or CPR face mask

(continued)

- Safety glasses (for first aiders)
- Safety pins
- Saline solution for eyes
- Sterile gauze pads—3-inch and 4-inch squares (preferably nonstick)
- Sterile gauze rolls
- Sunscreen—sun protection factor (SPF) 30 or greater
- Tape adherent and tape remover
- Tongue depressors
- Tooth saver kit
- Triangular bandages
- Tweezers

Adapted, by permission, from M. Flegel, 2004, *Sport first aid,* 3rd ed. (Champaign, IL: Human Kinetics), 20.

Emergency Action Plan

An emergency action plan is the final step in being prepared to take appropriate action for severe or serious injuries. The plan has three steps:

1. *Evaluate the injured player.*

   Use your CPR and first aid training to guide you. Be sure to keep these certifications up to date. Practice your skills frequently to keep them fresh and ready to use if and when you need them.

2. *Call the appropriate medical personnel.*

   If possible, delegate the responsibility of seeking medical help to another calm and responsible adult who attends all practices and matches. Write out a list of emergency phone numbers and keep it with you at practices and matches. Include the phone numbers for the following:

   - Rescue unit
   - Hospital
   - Physician
   - Police
   - Fire department

   Take each athlete's emergency information to every practice and game (see Emergency Information Card in appendix A on page 157). This information includes the person to contact in case of an emergency, what types of medications the athlete is using, what types of drugs the athlete is allergic to, and so on.

   Give an emergency response card (see Emergency Response Card in appendix A on page 158) to the contact person calling for emergency assistance. Having this information ready should help the contact person remain calm. You must also complete an injury report form (see page 156 in appendix A) and keep it on file for any injury that occurs.

3. *Provide first aid.*

   If medical personnel are not on hand at the time of the injury, you should provide first aid care to the extent of your qualifications. Again, although your CPR and first aid training will guide you, it is important to remember the following:

   - Do not move the injured athlete if the injury is to the head, neck, or back; if a large joint (ankle, knee, elbow, shoulder) is dislocated; or if the pelvis, a rib, or an arm or leg is fractured.
   - Calm the injured athlete and keep others away from her as much as possible.
   - Evaluate whether the athlete's breathing has stopped or is irregular, and if necessary, clear the airway with your fingers.
   - Administer CPR as directed in the CPR certification course recommended by your school, league, or state association.
   - Remain with the athlete until medical personnel arrive.

Steps to Take in an Emergency

Because every second counts in an emergency, be sure you have a clear, well-rehearsed emergency action plan. Your plan should follow this sequence:

1. Check the athlete's level of consciousness.
2. Send a contact person to call the appropriate medical personnel and the athlete's parents.
3. Send someone to wait for the medical personnel and direct them to the injured athlete.
4. Assess the injury.
5. Administer first aid.
6. Assist emergency medical personnel in preparing the athlete for transportation to a medical facility.
7. Appoint someone to go with the athlete if a parent is not available. This person should be responsible, calm, and familiar with the athlete. Assistant coaches or parents are best for this job.
8. Complete an injury report form while the incident is fresh in your mind (see page 156 in appendix A).

Taking Appropriate Action

Proper CPR and first aid training, a well-stocked first aid kit, and an emergency action plan help prepare you to take appropriate action when an injury occurs. We spoke in the previous section about the importance of providing first aid to the extent of your qualifications. Don't "play doctor" with injuries; sort out minor injuries that you can treat from those that need medical attention. Now let's look at taking the appropriate action for minor injuries and more serious injuries.

Minor Injuries

Although no injury seems minor to the person experiencing it, most injuries are neither life threatening nor severe enough to restrict participation. When these injuries occur, you can take an active role in their initial treatment.

Scrapes and Cuts When one of your players has an open wound, the first thing you should do is put on a pair of disposable latex-free examination gloves or some other effective blood barrier. Then follow these four steps:

1. Stop the bleeding by applying direct pressure with a clean dressing to the wound and elevating it. The player may be able to apply this pressure while you put on your gloves. Do not remove the dressing if it becomes soaked with blood. Instead, place an additional dressing on top of the one already in place. If bleeding continues, elevate the injured area above the heart and maintain pressure.
2. Cleanse the wound thoroughly once the bleeding is controlled. A good rinsing with a forceful stream of water, and perhaps light scrubbing with soap, will help prevent infection.
3. Protect the wound with sterile gauze or a bandage strip. If the player continues to participate, apply protective padding over the injured area.
4. Remove and dispose of gloves carefully to prevent you or anyone else from coming into contact with blood.

For bloody noses not associated with serious facial injury, have the athlete sit and lean slightly forward. Then pinch the player's nostrils shut. If the bleeding continues after several minutes, or if the athlete has a history of nosebleeds, seek medical assistance.

Coaching Tip

You shouldn't let a fear of acquired immune deficiency syndrome (AIDS) and other communicable diseases stop you from helping a player. You are at risk only if you allow contaminated blood to come in contact with an open wound on your body, so the examination gloves that you wear will protect you from AIDS should one of your players carry this disease. Check with your sport director, your league, or the Centers for Disease Control and Prevention (CDC) for more information about protecting yourself and your participants from AIDS.

Strains and Sprains The physical demands of tennis training and matches often result in injury to the muscles or tendons (strains) or to the ligaments (sprains). When your players suffer minor strains or sprains, immediately apply the PRICE method of injury care:

P **Protect the athlete and injured body part from further danger or trauma.**

R **Rest the area to avoid further damage and to foster healing.**

I **Ice the area to reduce swelling and pain.**

C **Compress the area by securing an ice bag in place with an elastic wrap.**

E **Elevate the injury above heart level to keep the blood from pooling in the area.**

Bumps and Bruises Inevitably, tennis players make contact with the ground. If the force applied to a body part at impact is great enough, a bump or bruise will result. Many players continue playing with such sore spots, but if the bump or bruise is large and painful, you should act appropriately. Again, use the PRICE method for injury care and monitor the injury. If swelling, discoloration, and pain have lessened, the player may resume participation with protective padding; if not, the player should be examined by a physician.

Serious Injuries

Head, neck, and back injuries; fractures; and injuries that cause a player to lose consciousness are among a class of injuries that you cannot and should not try to treat yourself. In these cases you should follow the emergency action plan outlined on pages 42 and 43. We do want to examine more closely, however, your role in preventing and attending to heat cramps, heat exhaustion, and heatstroke. Additionally, figure 4.2 illustrates the signs and symptoms associated with heat exhaustion and heatstroke.

Heat Cramps Tough practices combined with heat stress and substantial fluid loss from sweating can result in muscle cramps commonly known as heat cramps. Cramping (a tightening of the muscle) is most common when the weather is hot. Depending on your location, it may be hot early in the season, which can be problematic because players may be less conditioned and less adapted to heat, or later in the season, when players are better conditioned but still not used to playing in high temperatures. A severe enough cramp can prevent athletes from playing.

Dehydration, electrolyte loss, and fatigue are the contributing factors to cramping. The immediate treatment is to have the player cool off, replace fluids lost through activity, and slowly stretch the contracted muscle. The player may return to play later that same day or the next day provided the cramp doesn't cause a muscle strain.

Figure 4.2 Signs and symptoms of heat exhaustion and heatstroke.

Heat Exhaustion Heat exhaustion is a shocklike condition caused by strenuous activity combined with heat stress. This, in addition to dehydration and electrolyte depletion, results in symptoms that include dizziness, headache, fatigue, profuse sweating, nausea, vomiting, diarrhea, and muscle cramps. Difficulty with maintaining activity level and a mildly increased body temperature are key signs of heat exhaustion.

A player suffering from heat exhaustion should rest in a cool (shaded or air-conditioned) area with the legs propped above heart level; remove excess clothing and equipment; drink cool fluids, particularly those containing electrolytes (if not nauseated); and apply ice to the neck, back, or abdomen to help cool the body. If you believe a player is suffering from heat exhaustion, seek medical attention. Under no conditions should the player return to activity that day, and it is recommended that she not return to activity without a written release from her physician.

Heatstroke Heatstroke is a life-threatening condition in which the body stops sweating and body temperature rises dangerously high as a result of strenuous activity in extreme temperatures. It occurs when dehydration and electrolyte depletion cause a malfunction in the body's temperature control center in the brain. Symptoms include dizziness, headache, fatigue, disorientation, irritability, nausea, vomiting, diarrhea, and the feeling of being extremely hot. Key signs include severely increased body temperature, skin that is either hot and wet or completely dry, rapid pulse, rapid breathing, seizures, unconsciousness, and respiratory or cardiac arrest.

If you suspect a player is suffering from heatstroke, send for emergency medical assistance immediately and cool the player as quickly as possible. Remove excess clothing and equipment and cool the player's body with cool, wet towels; by pouring cool water over him; or by placing him in a cold bath. Apply ice packs to the armpits, neck, back, and abdomen and between his legs. If the player is conscious, give him cool fluids to drink. If he is unconscious or falls unconscious, place him on his side to allow fluids and vomit to drain from his mouth. A player who has suffered heatstroke should not be permitted to return to the team without a written release from a physician.

Protecting Yourself

When one of your players is injured, naturally your first concern is the player's well-being. Your desire to help youngsters, after all, was what made you decide to coach. Unfortunately, you must consider something else: Can you be held liable for the injury?

From a legal standpoint, a coach must fulfill nine duties. We've discussed all but planning in this chapter (which will be discussed in chapters 5 and 10). The following is a summary of your legal duties:

1. Provide a safe environment.
2. Plan the activity properly.
3. Provide adequate and proper equipment.
4. Match athletes appropriately.
5. Warn athletes and their parents of the risks inherent in the sport.
6. Supervise the activity closely.
7. Evaluate athletes for injury or incapacitation.
8. Know emergency procedures, CPR, and first aid.
9. Keep adequate records.

In addition to fulfilling these nine legal duties, you should check your organization's insurance coverage and your own personal insurance coverage to make sure these policies will properly protect you from liability.

5

Making Practices Fun and Practical

In the past, coaches have placed too much emphasis on learning skills and not enough on learning how to play skillfully—that is, how to use those skills in competition. The games approach, in contrast to the traditional approach, emphasizes learning what to do first, then how to do it. Moreover, the games approach lets kids discover what to do in the game not by your telling them, but by their experiencing it. It is a guided discovery method of teaching that empowers kids to solve the problems that arise in the game, which is a large part of the fun in learning.

On the surface, it would seem to make sense to introduce tennis by first teaching the basic skills of the sport and then the tactics of the game (the traditional approach), but it has been discovered that this approach has disadvantages. First, it teaches the skills of the sport out of the context of the game. Kids may learn to serve and hit forehand and backhand ground strokes, but they find it difficult to use these skills in the real game. This is because they do not yet understand the basic tactical skills of tennis and do not appreciate how best to use their newfound technical skills in actual competition. Second, learning skills by doing drills outside of the context of the game is downright boring. The single biggest turnoff in sports is overorganized instruction that deprives kids of their intrinsic desire to play the game.

The games approach, however, uses a four-step process:

1. Play a modified game.
2. Help players understand the game.
3. Teach the skills of the game.
4. Practice the skills in another game.

Step 1: Play a Modified Game

It's the first day of practice; some of the kids are eager to get started, while others are obviously apprehensive. Some have rarely hit a ball, and most don't know the rules. What do you do?

Using the traditional approach, you would start with a quick warm-up activity; then line the players up for a simple ground stroke drill and go from there. Using the games approach, however, you begin by having the players play a modified game that is developmentally appropriate for their level and also designed to focus on learning a specific part of the game.

Modifying the game allows you to emphasize a limited number of game situations. This is one way you "guide" your players to discover certain tactics in the game. For instance, you may have your players play a game in which the object is to just get the ball over the net and into the court consistently. Such a game forces them to think about what they have to do to get the ball over the net.

Drill Checklist

When developing matchlike drills for your youth tennis program, ask yourself these questions:

- Are the drills fun?
- Are the drills organized?
- Are the players involved in the drills?
- Is creativity and decision making being used?
- Are the spaces used appropriate?
- Is my feedback appropriate?
- Are there implications for the game?

Step 2: Help Players Understand the Game

As your players are playing a game, look for the right spot to "freeze" the action, step in, and ask questions about errors that you're seeing. When you do this, you help them better understand the objective of the game, what it is they must do to achieve that objective, and also what skills they must use to achieve that objective.

Asking the right questions is a very important part of your teaching. Essentially, you'll be asking your players—usually literally—"What do you need to do to succeed in this situation?" Sometimes players simply need to have more time playing the game, or you may need to modify the game further to make it easier for them to discover what they need to do. It may take more patience on your part, but it's a powerful way to learn. For example, assume your players are playing a game in which the objective is to hit the ball crosscourt over the net using a forehand ground stroke, but they are having trouble doing so. Interrupt the action and ask the following questions:

- What are you supposed to do in this game?
- What do you have to do to hit the ball using a forehand ground stroke?
- What do you do differently for a crosscourt forehand ground stroke versus down the line?
- When do you need to hit the ball to direct it crosscourt versus down the line?

Coaching Tip

If your players have trouble understanding what to do, phrase your question to let them choose between two options. For example, if you ask them, "What's the best way to hit the ball with consistency?" and get answers such as, "As hard as you can," then ask, "Do you use the sweet spot of your racket or the edge?"

At first, asking the right questions might seem difficult because your players have little or no experience with the game. And, if you've learned sport through the traditional approach, you'll be tempted to tell your players how to play the game rather than wasting time asking questions. In the games approach, however, you must resist this powerful temptation to tell your players what to do.

Instead, through modified games and skillful questioning on your part, your players should come to the realization on their own that hitting early or late determines the direction of the shot and can be used to make an opponent move side to side. Just as important, as you can see, rather than telling them what the critical skills are, you led them to this discovery, which is a crucial part of the games approach.

Step 3: Teach the Skills of the Game

Only when your players recognize the skills they need to be successful in the game do you want to teach the specific skills through focused activities. This is when you use a more traditional approach to teaching sport skills, the IDEA approach, which we describe in chapter 6. This type of teaching breaks down the skills of the game. Implement it early in the season so players can begin attaining skill, which will make games more fun.

Step 4: Practice the Skills in Another Game

As a coach, you want your players to experience success as they're learning skills. The best way to ensure that your players experience success early on is to create an advantage for them. Once they have practiced the skill, as outlined in step 3, put them in another game situation—this time emphasizing the advantage of the skill they've just learned. For example, you can emphasize crosscourt ground strokes when rallying from behind the baseline by having one player hit only crosscourt shots while the other hits only down-the-line shots.

We recommend first using a normal game situation (e.g., both players rally from the baseline using either crosscourt or down-the-line forehand ground strokes) and then introducing games in which one player hits crosscourt while the other hits down the line. This will introduce players to situations they will experience in competition and let them discover the challenges of performing the necessary skill. Then you teach them the skill, have them practice it, and put them back in another game—this time using an advantage to give them a greater chance of experiencing success.

As players improve their skills, however, you may not need to provide an advantage. For example, hitting only crosscourt shots can be very predictable. Your players need to understand that to end the point they may need to hit down the line on a short ball. In essence, they must learn to hit both types of shots and understand the situations in which each is used. When this time comes, you can lessen the advantage, or you may even decide that they're ready to practice the skill in regular competition. The key is to set up situations in which your athletes experience success, yet are challenged in doing so. This will take careful monitoring on your part, but having kids play altered games as they are learning skills is a very effective way of helping them learn and improve.

Using the games approach, your players will get to play more in practice. Once they learn how the skills fit into their performance and enjoyment of the game, they'll be more motivated to work on those skills, which will help them to be successful.

Coaching Tip

Some tennis skills don't lend themselves easily to providing an advantage. For example, the basic mechanics of hitting with topspin on ground strokes, hitting a slice serve, and playing half volleys are best learned with as much individual attention from the coach as possible, often as players practice with partners. Practicing offensive and defensive tactics, however, is more ideal in a matchlike setting.

6

Teaching and Shaping Skills

Coaching tennis is about teaching kids how to play the game by teaching them skills, fitness concepts, and values. It's also about coaching players before, during, and after matches. Teaching and coaching are closely related, but there are important differences. In this chapter we focus on principles of teaching, especially on teaching technical and tactical skills. But these principles apply to teaching fitness concepts and values as well. Armed with these principles, you will be able to design effective and efficient practices and will understand how to deal with misbehavior. Then you will be able to teach the skills necessary to be successful in tennis that are outlined in chapters 7 and 8.

Teaching Tennis Skills

Many people believe that the only qualification needed to teach a skill is to have performed it. Although having performed a skill is helpful, teaching it successfully requires much more than that. And even if you haven't performed the skill, you can still learn to teach successfully with the useful acronym IDEA:

I Introduce the skill.

D Demonstrate the skill.

E Explain the skill.

A Attend to players practicing the skill.

Introduce the Skill

Players, especially those who are young and inexperienced, need to know what skill they are learning and why they are learning it. You should therefore use the following three steps every time you introduce a skill to your players:

1. Get your players' attention.
2. Name the skill.
3. Explain the importance of the skill.

Get Your Players' Attention

Because youngsters are easily distracted, you must often do something to get their attention. Some coaches use interesting news items or stories. Others use jokes. Still others simply project enthusiasm to get their players to listen. Whatever method you use, speak slightly above your normal volume and look your players in the eye when you speak.

Also, position players so they can see and hear you. Arrange them in two or three evenly spaced rows, facing you. (Make sure they aren't looking into the sun or at a distracting activity.) Then ask whether all of them can see you before you begin to speak.

Coaching Tip
Writing out in detail each skill you will teach clarifies what you will say and how you will demonstrate and teach it. In addition, when you teach a skill, it is helpful to explain when the skill is used in the context of the game.

Name the Skill

Although there may be many common names for the skill you are introducing, decide as a staff before the start of the season which one you'll use and stick with it. This will help prevent confusion and enhance communication among your players. When you introduce the new skill, call it by name several times so that the players automatically correlate the name with the skill in later discussions.

Explain the Importance of the Skill

As Rainer Martens, the founder of the American Sport Education Program (ASEP), has said, "The most difficult aspect of coaching is this: Coaches must learn to let athletes learn. Sport skills should be taught so they have meaning to the child, not just meaning to the coach." Although the importance of a skill may be apparent to you, your players may be less able to see how the skill will help them become better tennis players. Offer them a reason for learning the skill, and describe how the skill relates to more advanced skills.

Demonstrate the Skill

The demonstration step is the most important part of teaching sport skills to players who may never have done anything closely resembling it. They need a picture, not just words, so they can see how the skill is performed. If you are unable to perform the skill correctly, ask an assistant coach, one of your players, or someone more skilled to perform the demonstration.

These tips will help make your demonstrations effective:

- Use correct form.
- Demonstrate the skill several times.
- Slow the action, if possible, during one or two performances so players can see every movement involved in the skill.
- Perform the skill at different angles so your players can get a full perspective of it.
- Demonstrate the skill with both sides of the body.

Explain the Skill

Players learn more effectively when they're given a brief explanation of the skill along with the demonstration. Use simple terms and, if possible, relate the skill to previously learned skills. Ask your players whether they understand

Coaching Tip

Technology improvements have created an opportunity to bring new demonstration methods to the practice courts. If you have difficulty demonstrating a particular skill or locating someone who can demonstrate it for you, consider using some of the tennis skill DVDs and tennis magazines that are on the market. These can be especially effective with older players, who are better able to transfer such visual examples to their own performance than younger players are.

your description. A good technique is to ask the team to repeat your explanation. Ask questions such as, "What are you going to do first?" and "Then what?" If players look confused or uncertain, repeat your explanation and demonstration. If possible, use different words so your players get a chance to try to understand the skill from a different perspective.

Complex skills often are better understood when they are explained in more manageable parts. For instance, to teach your players how to hit an overhead shot, follow these steps:

1. Show players a correct performance of the entire skill and explain its function in tennis.
2. Break down the skill into component parts.
3. Have players perform each of the component parts of the skill, such as holding the racket, getting to the net, positioning the body, and hitting the overhead shot.
4. After players have demonstrated their ability to perform the separate parts of the skill in sequence, reexplain the entire skill.
5. Have players practice the entire skill in matchlike conditions.

How to Run Your Drills Properly

Before running a drill that teaches technique, do the following:

- Name the drill.
- Explain the skill or skills to be taught.
- Position the players correctly.
- Explain what the drill will accomplish.
- State the command that will start the drill, such as a whistle.
- State the command that will end the drill, such as a whistle.

Once you have introduced the drill and repeated it a few times in this manner, you will find that merely calling out the name of the drill is sufficient. Your players will automatically line up in the proper position to run the drill and practice the skill.

Because young players have short attention spans, a long demonstration or explanation of a skill may cause them to lose focus. Therefore, spend no more than a few minutes altogether on the introduction, demonstration, and explanation phases. Then involve the players in matchlike drills that call on them to perform the skill.

Attend to Players Practicing the Skill

If the skill you selected was within your players' capabilities and you have done an effective job of introducing, demonstrating, and explaining it, your players should be ready to attempt the skill. Some players, especially those in younger age groups, may need to be physically guided through the movements during their first few attempts. Walking unsure athletes through the skill in this way will help them gain confidence to perform the skill on their own.

Your teaching duties, though, don't end when all your athletes have demonstrated that they understand how to perform a skill. In fact, your teaching role is just beginning as you help your players improve their skills. A significant part of your teaching consists of closely observing the hit-and-miss trial performances of your players. You will shape players' skills by detecting errors and correcting them using positive feedback. Keep in mind that your positive feedback will have a great influence on your players' motivation to practice and improve their performances.

Remember, too, that some players may need individual instruction. So set aside a time before, during, or after practice to give individual help.

Helping Players Improve Skills

After you have successfully taught your players the fundamentals of a skill, your focus will be on helping them improve it. Players learn skills and improve them at different rates, so don't get frustrated if progress seems slow. Instead, help them improve by shaping their skills and detecting and correcting errors.

Shaping Players' Skills

One of your principal teaching duties is to reward positive effort and behavior—in terms of successful skill execution—when you see it. If a player makes a good hit in practice, immediately say, "That's the way to drive through it! Good follow-through!" This, plus a smile and a thumbs-up gesture, goes a long way toward reinforcing that technique in that player. However, sometimes you may have a long dry spell before you see correct techniques to reinforce. It's difficult to reward players when they don't execute skills correctly. How can you shape their skills if this is the case?

Shaping skills takes practice on your players' part and patience on yours. Expect your players to make errors. Telling the player who made the good hit that she did a good job doesn't ensure that she'll have the same success next time. Seeing inconsistency in your players' technique can be frustrating. It's even more challenging to stay positive when your athletes repeatedly perform a skill incorrectly or have a lack of enthusiasm for learning. It can certainly be frustrating to see athletes who seemingly don't heed your advice and continue to make the same mistakes.

It is normal to get frustrated sometimes when teaching skills. Nevertheless, part of successful coaching is controlling this frustration. Instead of getting upset, use these six guidelines for shaping skills:

1. *Think small initially.*

   Reward the first signs of behavior that approximate what you want. Then reward closer and closer approximations of the desired behavior. In short, use your reward power to shape the behavior you seek.

2. *Break skills into small steps.*

   For instance, in learning to serve, one of your players does well in tossing the ball, but he's hesitant with his swing and he doesn't hit the ball with full extension. He often hits the ball too far away from him as he serves, or when the ball is too low. Reinforce the correct technique of hitting with full extension, and teach him how to hit the ball at the height of the toss. Once he masters this, focus on getting him to control the placement of the ball.

3. *Develop one component of a skill at a time.*

   Don't try to shape two components of a skill at once. For example, in hitting a forehand, a player must get into position first and then hit the ball with the racket. Players should focus first on one aspect (getting into position), then on the other (hitting the ball with a forehand swing). Athletes often have problems mastering a skill because they're trying to improve two or more components at once. Help these athletes to isolate a single component.

4. *Use reinforcement only occasionally, for the best examples.*

   By focusing only on the best examples, you will help players continue to improve once they've mastered the basics. Using occasional reinforcement during practice allows players to have more time hitting the ball rather than having to constantly stop and listen to the coach. Tennis skills are best learned through a lot of repetition, such as matchlike drills. Make the best use of team practice time by allowing the players as much time hitting balls as possible.

5. *Relax your reward standards.*

   As players focus on mastering a new skill or attempt to integrate it with other skills, their old, well-learned skills may temporarily degenerate.

When this happens, you may need to relax your expectations. For example, a player has learned how to hit a slice serve with a basic serving motion and is now learning how to modify that technique to develop a new topspin serve. While the player is learning to adjust the grip and getting the timing and new motion down, both serves may be poor. A similar degeneration of skills may occur during growth spurts while the coordination of muscles, tendons, and ligaments catches up to the growth of bones. Lowering your expectations for the time being will give the athlete time to integrate the new skill or adjust to a growth spurt.

Coaching Tip
You can ask older players or those with advanced skill to "self-coach." With the proper guidance and a positive team environment, young players can think about how they perform a skill and make suggestions on their own of how they might be able to perform it better. Self-coaching is best done at practice, where a player can experiment with learning new skills.

6. *Go back to the basics.*

   If a well-learned skill degenerates for a long period of time, you may need to restore it by going back to the basics. If necessary, have the player practice the skill using an activity with less pressure from opponents (for example, have the player practice serves using targets and add a return player only when the player is comfortable with the new serve).

Detecting and Correcting Errors

Good coaches recognize that athletes make two types of errors: learning errors and performance errors. Learning errors are ones that occur because athletes don't know how to perform a skill; that is, they have not yet developed the correct motor pattern in the brain to perform the skill. Performance errors are made not because athletes don't know how to execute the skill, but because they have made a mistake in executing what they do know. There is no easy way to know whether a player is making a learning or performance error, and part of the art of coaching is being able to sort out which is which.

The process of helping your athletes correct errors begins with observing and evaluating their performances to determine whether the mistakes are learning or performance errors. Carefully watch your athletes to see if they routinely make the errors in both practice and match settings, or if the errors tend to occur only in match settings. If the latter is the case, then your athletes are making performance errors. For performance errors, you need to look for the reasons your athletes are not performing as well as they can. Perhaps they are nervous, or they get distracted by the match setting. If the mistakes are learning errors, then you need to help them learn the skill, which is the focus of this section.

When correcting learning errors, there is no substitute for knowing skills well. The better you understand a skill—not only how to perform it correctly but also what causes learning errors—the more helpful you will be in correcting players' mistakes.

One of the most common coaching mistakes is to provide inaccurate feedback and advice on how to correct errors. Don't rush into error correction; wrong feedback or poor advice will hurt the learning process more than no feedback or advice at all. If you are uncertain about the cause of the problem or how to correct it, continue to observe and analyze until you are more certain. As a rule, you should see the error repeated several times before attempting to correct it.

Correct One Error at a Time

Suppose Megan, one of your players, is having trouble with her backhand. She's doing most things well, but you notice that she's not stepping forward as she prepares to strike the ball, and she often stands still, not moving to the ball. What do you do?

First, decide which error to correct first, because athletes learn more effectively when they attempt to correct one error at a time. Determine whether one error is causing the other; if so, have the athlete correct that error first, because it may eliminate the other error. In Megan's case, however, neither error is causing the other. In such cases, athletes should correct the error that is easiest to correct and will bring the greatest improvement when remedied. For Megan, this probably means moving to meet the ball. Once she improves her ability to move to the ball and get in proper position, then work on her step forward. Note that improvement in the first area may even motivate her to correct the other error.

Use Positive Feedback to Correct Errors

The positive approach to correcting errors includes emphasizing what to do instead of what not to do. Use compliments, praise, rewards, and encouragement to correct errors. Acknowledge correct performance as well as efforts to improve. By using positive feedback, you can help your athletes feel good about themselves and promote a strong desire to achieve.

When you're working with one athlete at a time, the positive approach to correcting errors includes four steps:

1. *Praise effort and correct performance.*

   Praise the athlete for trying to perform a skill correctly and for performing any parts of it correctly. Praise the athlete immediately after he performs the skill, if possible. Keep the praise simple: "That's the way to stay balanced through the shot," "Way to hustle," "That shot had better spin," "Good extension," or "That's the way to follow through." You can also use nonverbal feedback, such as smiling, clapping your hands, or any facial or body expression that shows approval.

   Make sure you're sincere with your praise. Don't indicate that an athlete's effort was good when it wasn't. Usually an athlete knows when he has made a sincere effort to perform the skill correctly and perceives undeserved praise for what it is—untruthful feedback to make him feel good. Likewise, don't indicate that a player's performance was correct when it wasn't.

2. *Give simple and precise feedback to correct errors.*

   Don't burden a player with a long or detailed explanation of how to correct an error. Give just enough feedback so that the player can correct one error at a time. Before giving feedback, recognize that some athletes readily accept it immediately after the error; others will respond better if you delay the correction slightly.

   For errors that are complicated to explain and difficult to correct, try the following:

   - Do not demonstrate what the athlete did wrong. Instead, explain and demonstrate what the athlete should have done. For example, "By the time the ball bounces on your side of the net, your shoulder should be turned sideways."
   - Explain the cause or causes of the error, if they aren't obvious.
   - Explain why you are recommending the correction you have selected, if it's not obvious.

3. *Make sure the athlete understands your feedback.*

   If the athlete doesn't understand your feedback, she won't be able to correct the error. Ask her to repeat the feedback and to explain and demonstrate how she will use it. If the athlete can't do this, be patient and present your feedback again. Then have the athlete repeat the feedback after you're finished.

4. *Provide an environment that motivates the athlete to improve.*

   Your players won't always be able to correct their errors immediately even if they do understand your feedback. Encourage them to "hang tough" and stick with it when corrections are difficult or they seem discouraged. For more difficult corrections, remind them that it will take time and that improvement will happen only if they work at it. Encourage players with little self-confidence. Saying something like, "You were getting in position and using nice form to hit forehands today; with practice, you'll be able to accelerate your racket head and put more pace on the ball," can motivate a player to continue to refine his ground strokes.

   Other players may be very self-motivated and need little help from you in this area; with them you can practically ignore step 4 when correcting an error. Although motivation comes from within, try to provide an environment of positive instruction and encouragement to help your athletes improve.

Dealing With Misbehavior

Young athletes will misbehave at times; it's only natural. You can respond to misbehavior in one of two ways: through extinction or discipline.

Extinction

Ignoring a misbehavior—neither rewarding nor disciplining it—is called extinction. This can be effective under certain circumstances. In some situations, disciplining young people's misbehavior only encourages them to act up further because of the recognition they get. Ignoring misbehavior teaches youngsters that it is not worth your attention.

Sometimes, though, you cannot wait for a behavior to fizzle out. When players cause danger to themselves or others or disrupt the activities of others, you need to take immediate action. Tell the offending player that the behavior must stop and that discipline will follow if it doesn't. If the athlete doesn't stop misbehaving after the warning, use discipline.

Extinction also doesn't work well when a misbehavior is self-rewarding. For example, you may be able to keep from grimacing if a youngster kicks you in the shin, but even so, she still knows you were hurt. Therein lies the reward. In these circumstances, it is necessary to discipline the player for the undesirable behavior.

Extinction works best in situations in which players are seeking recognition through mischievous behaviors, clowning, or grandstanding. Usually, if you are patient, their failure to get your attention will cause the behavior to disappear. However, be alert that you don't extinguish desirable behavior. When youngsters do something well, they expect to be positively reinforced. Not rewarding them will likely cause them to discontinue the desired behavior.

Discipline

Some educators say we should never discipline young people, but should only reinforce their positive behaviors. They argue that discipline does not work, creates hostility, and sometimes develops avoidance behaviors that may be more unwholesome than the original problem behavior. It is true that discipline does not always work and that it can create problems when used ineffectively, but when used appropriately, discipline is effective in eliminating undesirable behaviors without creating other undesirable consequences. You must use discipline effectively, because it is impossible to guide athletes through positive reinforcement and extinction alone. Discipline is part of a positive approach when these guidelines are followed:

- Discipline in a corrective way to help athletes improve now and in the future. Don't discipline to retaliate and make yourself feel better.

- Impose discipline in an impersonal way when athletes break team rules or otherwise misbehave. Shouting at or scolding athletes indicates that your attitude is one of revenge.
- Once a good rule has been agreed on, ensure that athletes who violate it experience the unpleasant consequences of their misbehavior. Don't wave discipline threateningly over their heads. Just do it, but warn an athlete once before disciplining.
- Be consistent in administering discipline.
- Don't discipline using consequences that may cause you guilt. If you can't think of an appropriate consequence right away, tell the player you will talk with him after you think about it. You might consider involving the player in designing a consequence.
- Once the discipline is completed, don't make athletes feel that they are "in the doghouse." Always make them feel that they're valued members of the team.
- Make sure that what you think is discipline isn't perceived by the athlete as desirable; for instance, excluding a player from a certain activity or portion of the training session may be just what the athlete desired.
- Never discipline athletes for making errors when they are playing.
- Never use physical activity—running laps or doing push-ups—as discipline. Doing so only causes athletes to resent physical activity, something we want them to learn to enjoy throughout their lives.
- Discipline sparingly. Constant discipline and criticism cause athletes to turn their interests elsewhere and to resent you as well.

Coaching Tip

Involve older athletes in the process of setting team rules and determining the consequences for breaking them. Older or more experienced players can be capable of brainstorming ideas for discipline in common situations such as being late to practice, criticizing another player, or talking back to the coach. Once you've agreed on a list of rules and consequences, have all players sign the rules to cement their willingness to abide by them.

7

Coaching Basic Tennis Skills

This chapter focuses on the basic skills your players need to perform effectively in youth tennis. Remember to use the IDEA approach to teaching skills: introduce, demonstrate, and explain the skill, and attend to players as they practice the skill (see page 56 in chapter 6). This chapter also ties directly into the season and practice plans in chapter 10, describing the skills you'll teach at the practices outlined there. If you aren't familiar with tennis skills, you may find it helpful to watch a video so you can see the skills performed correctly. Additionally, because the information in this book is limited to tennis basics, you will need to advance your knowledge as a coach as your players advance in their skills. You can do this by learning from your experiences, watching and talking with more experienced coaches, and studying resources on advanced skills.

The tennis skills you will teach your players at the youth level are basic racket-handling and rallying skills. You will also teach them about court positioning and the various shots they will use based on their positions on the court. Mastering these techniques will allow your players to better execute specific shots during the game. These basic skills serve as the foundation for playing tennis well at all levels.

Racket-Handling Skills

As you may know, the most basic skill in tennis is the stroke, also known as the swing. The purpose of the stroke is to get the ball over the net and into the opponent's court. Although this skill is simple in concept, it can be difficult to execute. Players must develop a feel for the racket and learn how their grip on the racket, their contact of the ball, and their control of the ball off the racket contribute to the shot.

Grip

The grip a player uses on the handle of the racket determines the racket-face angle at the point of contact based on the position of the player's hand, wrist, and arm. Your players must use the proper grip for each stroke they make on the court. To choose the proper grip, players need to consider several factors, such as the speed, height, bounce, and spin of the ball, and their position on the court.

Before teaching your players the various grips, which are described in the following text, be sure they know how to properly hold the racket, as shown in figure 7.1. The player should hold the racket by the handle, with the hand on the grip area (see figure 3.3 on page 24 for more information on the parts of a racket). The racket is held with three fingers at the end of the handle followed by the thumb, which overlaps the middle finger. The index finger is positioned near the top of the handle and slightly separated from the thumb.

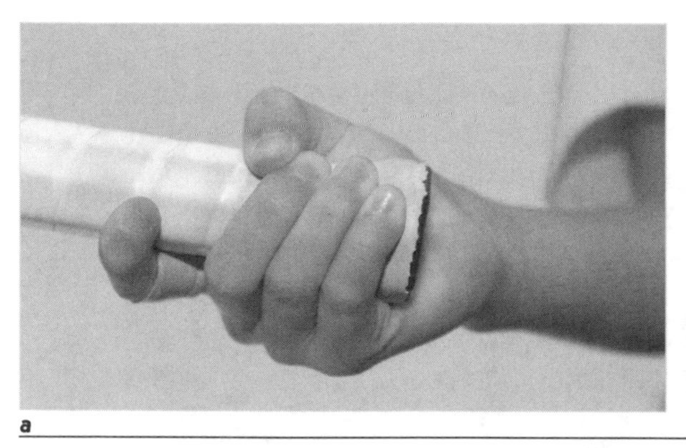

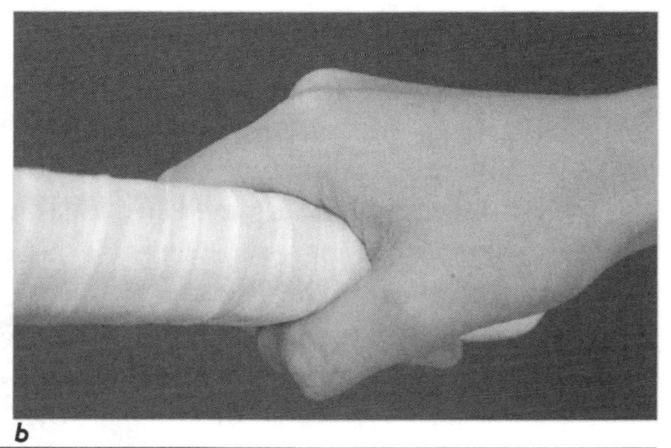

a b

Figure 7.1 Holding a racket.

Playing Forehands and Backhands

All of the shots you will learn about in this chapter can be hit either forehand or backhand. A forehand shot is played on the dominant side of the body. As the ball comes over the net, the player hits it as though he were using the palm of his hand (see figure 7.2*a*). The backhand is hit on the nondominant side of the body, using either one or two hands, as you will learn later in this chapter. As the ball comes over the net, the player hits it as though he were using the back side of the hand, similar to throwing a Frisbee (see figure 7.2*b*). A two-handed backhand is hit with both hands close together on the handle; the player hits as though he were using the palm of his nondominant hand.

a b

Figure 7.2 Example of *(a)* forehand and *(b)* backhand.

Continental Grip

The continental grip is a one-handed grip used for the serve and universally for both forehand and backhand volleys. It can also be used for ground strokes, but it is generally limited to very low balls that are hit with backspin, or defensive shots when net clearance is more important than power. This grip is also used for the serve because it allows the player to hit with spin. The position of the handle is offset to give the wrist the flexibility to hit with both power and spin. With the racket face perpendicular to the court, the player holds the handle with the dominant hand as though gripping a hammer (see figure 7.3).

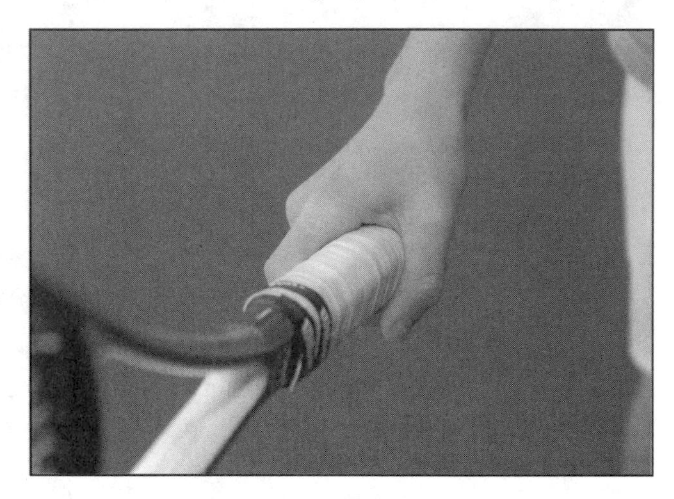

Figure 7.3 Continental grip.

Eastern Forehand Grip

The eastern forehand grip is a one-handed grip used on the forehand side for balls with no or moderate topspin when the contact point is between the player's knees and hips. With the racket face perpendicular to the court, the player holds the handle with the dominant hand; the palm is on the same plane as the racket face. The thumb and first finger form a V and are positioned directly on the top of the flat bevel that is parallel with the court surface (see figure 7.4).

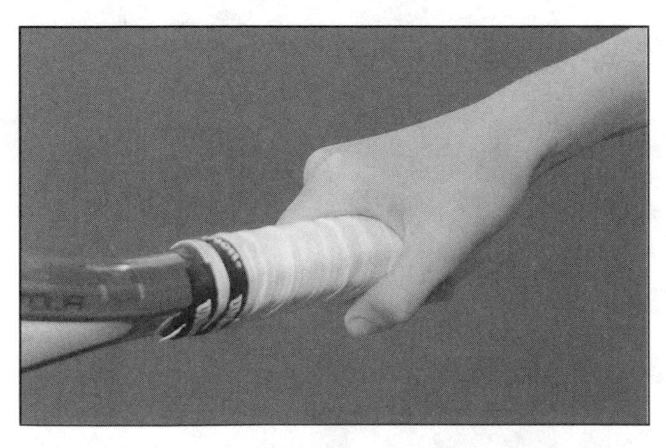

Figure 7.4 Eastern forehand grip.

Semi-Western Forehand Grip

The semi-western forehand grip is a one-handed grip used on the forehand side for balls with moderate to heavy topspin when the contact point is between the player's waist and shoulders. With the racket face perpendicular to the court, the palm is positioned slightly more under the handle than in the eastern forehand grip. The racket is held with the bottom three fingers, and the thumb overlaps the middle finger. The index finger is on top and is slightly separated from the thumb. For right-handed players, the V formed by the thumb and first finger is on the top right bevel as the player holds the racket perpendicular to the court (see figure 7.5).

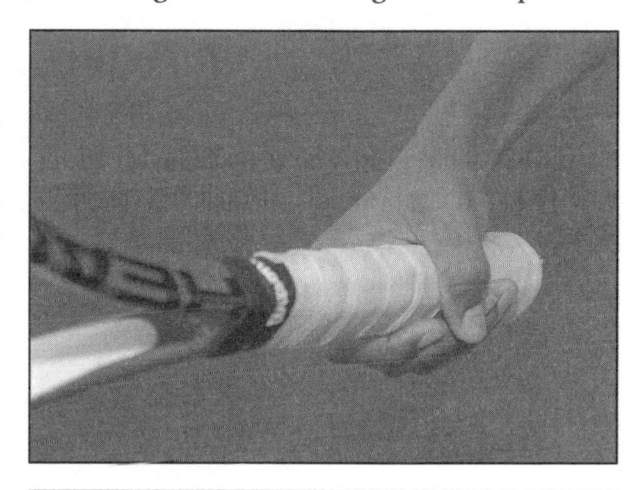

Figure 7.5 Semi-western forehand grip.

Western Forehand Grip

The western forehand grip is a one-handed grip used on the forehand side for balls with heavy topspin when the contact point is around shoulder height. This grip is not a good choice for low balls or when the racket face needs to be open for defensive shots. It is also a very poor grip for serves and volleys. For volleys, the racket face would be closed on the forehand side, and the hand and wrist would have to assume an awkward position to open the racket face to get the ball over the net. For serves, the racket would be directly behind the ball for a flat serve, and the handle would be in a direct line with the wrist so

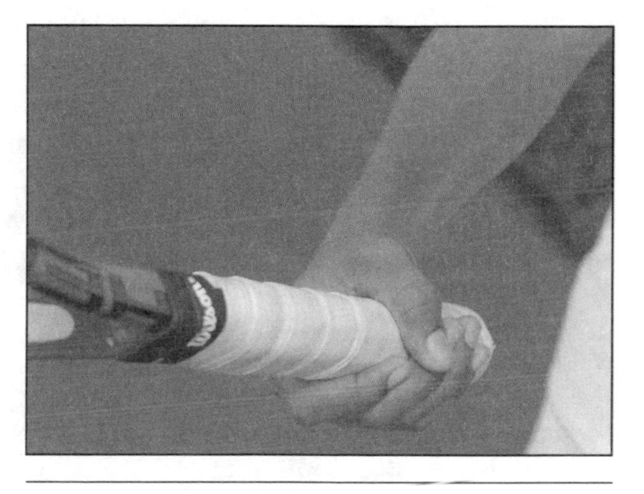

Figure 7.6 Western forehand grip.

it couldn't snap for power. The player would have to generate spin by turning the wrist around the ball at the contact point, causing the ball to curve right to left.

With the racket face perpendicular to the court, the palm is positioned under the handle, and the first finger and thumb form a V over the back flat bevel. This grip is sometimes called the frying pan grip because the hand is under the handle just as it would be when picking up a frying pan (see figure 7.6).

Eastern Backhand Grip

The eastern backhand grip is a one-handed grip used on the backhand side for balls with no to moderate topspin when the contact point is at waist level. With the racket face perpendicular to the court, the player grips the handle with the dominant hand so the base knuckle of the index finger is on the top bevel of the handle. Like the eastern forehand and continental grips, three fingers are at the bottom, followed by the thumb, which overlaps the middle finger. The index finger is separated from the thumb on top (see figure 7.7).

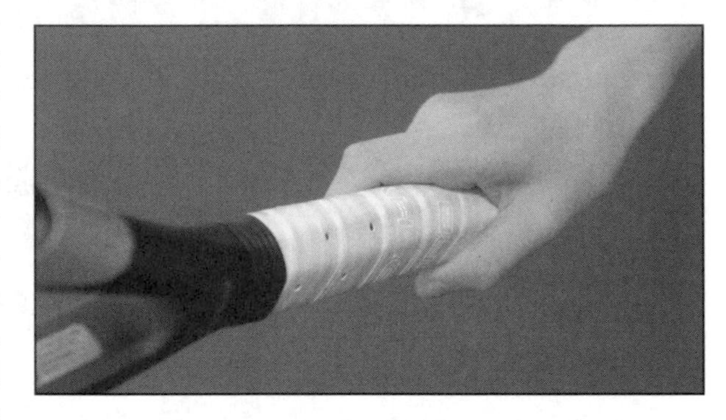

Figure 7.7 Eastern backhand grip.

Two-Handed Backhand Grip

The two-handed backhand grip is a two-handed grip used on the backhand side for balls with moderate to heavy topspin when the contact point is at waist level. This grip has a number of variations, but the strongest and most common variation used at the youth level is a semi-western forehand grip for the top hand (the nondominant hand) and a continental grip for the bottom hand (the dominant hand), as shown in figure 7.8. Certain shots, such as slice backhands, volleys, and defensive backhands, may require a farther reach than the player can make with a two-handed grip. In these situations, the player can drop the top hand off the racket and hit the ball using a one-handed backhand with the continental grip.

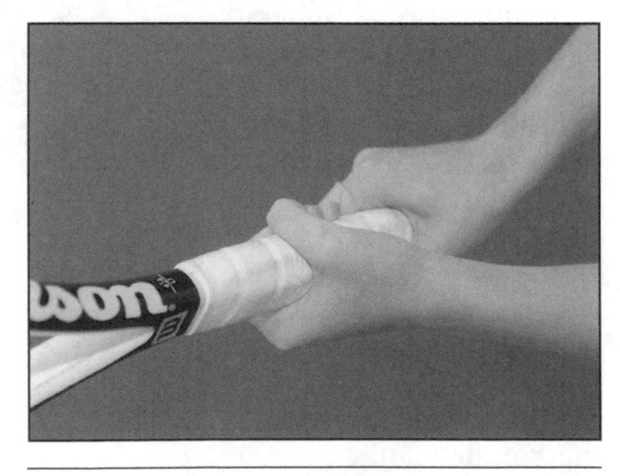

Figure 7.8 Two-handed backhand grip.

Contacting the Ball

The most important element of any tennis stroke is the contact point, the point—in both location and timing—at which the ball meets the face of the racket. Simply stated, the ball will go wherever the racket face is pointing at contact. To have optimum control of the ball, a player must have a consistent contact point. This is true in all sports—baseball players are most successful when they hit the ball in the middle of the strike zone, and golfers hit their best shots when the ground is level and the ball is on a tee. For tennis, specifically for a forehand ground stroke, the best contact point is about waist height, with the racket face even with the front foot and the hitting arm elbow held away from the body, as shown in figure 7.9.

Coaching Tip

As a general rule, teach your players that the faster the ball is approaching, the less backswing is necessary. Many young players believe that extra backswing is needed for power, but most often the longer backswing results in a ball hit too late for adequate control. Teach players to keep backswings short on hard-hit balls to ensure that the contact point is in front of the body.

Figure 7.9 Ideal contact point for a forehand ground stroke.

When players hit shots at the ideal contact point, they have more options for spin, power, and placement. When they strike the ball outside this contact point, swing patterns change and the ability to hit with various speeds, spins, and direction is limited. For example, if the ball is contacted too close to the body, the swing will be cramped and short and the racket angle tends to be open, resulting in a shot with little speed and a trajectory that makes the ball pop up and float. In addition, shots hit late, past the contact point, are often the result of an excessive backswing and lack power, spin, and control. Shots hit early, before the contact point, are generally hit across the body and go outside the boundary lines of the court.

P-A-S System

As your players learn how to handle their rackets, you may find it helpful to teach them the P-A-S system. This system is an easy way for novice coaches to explain the results of every shot, break down and teach specific skills, and correct players' mistakes.

Each stroke essentially has three characteristics that are simple to identify when observed independently. In the P-A-S system, the P represents the path—or swing pattern—of the racket, the A represents the angle of the racket at the point of contact, and the S represents the speed of the swing. Every stroke can be described using P-A-S, and errors can be detected and corrected using this simple system. To clarify, let's look at how the P-A-S system works for a few types of strokes (all of these strokes will be discussed in detail later in this chapter):

Topspin Backhand Ground Stroke

- *Path*—Low to high
- *Angle*—Perpendicular to the court
- *Speed*—Moderate to fast, depending on the speed of the shot

Forehand Drop Shot

- *Path*—High to level
- *Angle*—Open
- *Speed*—Slow

Forehand Lob

- *Path*—Low to high
- *Angle*—Open
- *Speed*—Medium

Controlling the Ball

Players at the youth level need to learn not only how to hit a ball over the net but also how to control the ball with the racket for proper shot placement. The five types of control are as follows:

1. Hitting right and left
2. Hitting high and low
3. Hitting short and deep
4. Hitting with spin
5. Hitting with power

Hitting Right and Left

The angle of the racket face at contact controls the direction of the ball right or left. Teach players how to contact the ball with the racket face pointed to the right (the ball will go right) and to the left (the ball will go left), as shown in figure 7.10. Then they'll be able to keep their opponents on the move. By simply changing the angle of the racket, players learn to direct the ball from one side of the court to the other and how to place the ball in different parts of the court. Have your players think about the advantages of moving their opponents from side to side and playing shots to opponents' weak sides.

a

b

Figure 7.10 Directing a ball *(a)* to the right and *(b)* to the left.

Hitting High and Low

To hit high and low, or control the height of the shot, players turn the racket face; this is called "opening" or "closing" the racket. As we learned previously, the direction of the ball is determined by the direction (right or left) the racket face is pointing at contact. The height of the shot, however, is determined by the direction (up or down) the racket face is angled at contact.

An open racket face, as shown in figure 7.11*a*, points toward the sky and allows a player to get the ball high enough to clear the net. A closed racket face, as shown in figure 7.11*b*, points toward the court and aims the ball directly into the net. Therefore, a closed racket face should not be used upon contact when hitting the ball. Rather, it is used during the backswing for shots such as topspin ground strokes. If a player's grip is in the proper position for the

Figure 7.11 *(a)* Open and *(b)* closed racket.

racket face to be perpendicular at contact, the racket face will naturally close slightly on the backswing. However, if the racket face is closed at contact, the ball will lack the upward trajectory for net clearance. Because most errors go into the net, a slightly open racket face will help ensure that the ball goes up and over the net and travels deeper in the court.

Hitting Short and Deep

Hitting short and deep requires a combination of speed, height over the net, and spin. When a ball is hit hard and high, it will travel deep in the court, helping to keep an opponent from attacking, or, in other words, moving toward the net. Players should be aware that there are many openings in the court that will force the opponent to run to get to the ball for the next shot. When the opponent is positioned deep in the court, these openings are on either side of the opponent (see figure 7.12*a*) or short and in front of the opponent. When the opponent is positioned at the net, the opening is deep in the court (see figure 7.12*b*).

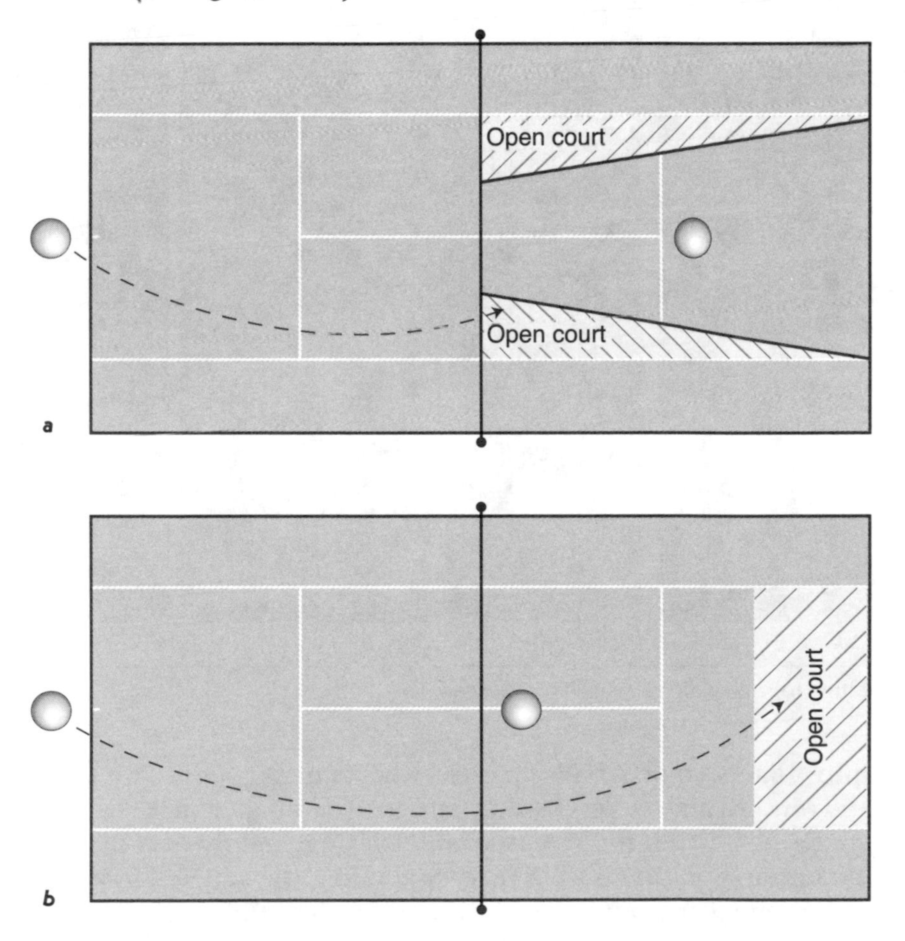

Figure 7.12 Openings in the court: *(a)* at the sides and *(b)* deep.

Hitting With Spin

The use of spin on the ball allows players to gain more control of their shots. Spin is a concept that should be introduced to all players, even beginners. By imparting various types of spin, players no longer have to rely solely on gravity to keep shots in the court. The two types of spin that you should introduce to youth players are topspin and backspin.

Topspin Topspin on a ball is created when a player brushes up behind the ball with the racket, using a low-to-high swing pattern (see figure 7.13). Topspin allows players to hit the ball harder and higher over the net because the forward rotation of the ball curves the shot down into the court. Topspin should be used for most ground strokes from the baseline because it allows for a safe net clearance, and the spin will pull the ball into the opponent's court.

Figure 7.13 Creating topspin with a low-to-high swing pattern.

Backspin Backspin on a ball is created when a player starts with the racket high and hits in a high-to-level swing pattern with an open racket face at contact (see figure 7.14). If hit hard, the ball will float and fly over the baseline before it bounces on the court. If hit easy and low, the ball will stay low after hitting the court. Backspin is generally used when hitting the ball short such as on drop shots or on approach shots in which players want the ball to stay low after the bounce. Backspin is also used on defensive shots when a player

a b c

Figure 7.14 Creating backspin with a high-to-level swing pattern.

is out of position and needs more trajectory on the shot for net clearance and more time to recover back into the court. The backspin will cause the ball to travel farther back in the court even when not hit hard so the player will have more recovery time.

Hitting With Power

A shot is more effective if the ball gets to the spot quickly, making it difficult for the opponent to return. The speed at which a ball travels is determined by the speed of the oncoming ball and the length and momentum of the swing used to strike the ball. When a player has ample time, a full swing with the body coiled so that the side of the body is to the net and the racket points to the back wall will impart maximum racket speed to the shot (see figure 7.15*a*). Swings that have more backswing, as shown in figure 7.15*b*, take more time and are difficult to control.

Note that the path of the swing also influences how fast the ball leaves the racket. A flat swing pattern that is parallel to the ground will give maximum power, but flat shots are difficult to control because there is no spin on the ball to help pull the ball down. A low-to-high swing pattern will generate topspin for control, but ball speed will be decreased.

> **Coaching Tip**
>
> You will find that some of your young players like to hit the ball hard. They should be aware, however, that as they increase the power of their strokes, they decrease their ability to control their shots. Good players must master the ability to hit with the first four controls (hitting right and left, high and low, short and deep, and with spin) before they attempt power.

Figure 7.15 Imparting power to the ball with the swing path: *(a)* correct and *(b)* incorrect.

Feeding the Ball

Feeding is a way to introduce the ball in play during practice. Teaching your players how to make "friendly feeds" to teammates allows you to move around the court to offer tips and suggestions. Feeding also helps players gain experience and confidence in handling the racket and ball. Each activity may require a different type of feed depending on the skill level of the player. The following feeds are listed in order from easy to more advanced.

- *Dropped ball from partner*—The feeder stands to the side and slightly in front of the hitter so that the ball is dropped at the contact point.
- *Self-dropped ball*—The player pushes the ball upward out of the hand and aims the ball to drop even with the front foot.
- *Tossed ball*—The feeder tosses the ball gently underhand, aiming at a target on the court that is about two-thirds of the distance between the two players.
- *Forehand feed*—The feeder chokes up on the racket to enhance control and reduce power and then self-drops and feeds to a target.

In general, design activities so that players are feeding to each other as they work on skills so that you can spend more time individually with your players and are not restricted to the ball basket and the task of feeding. If your players' feeds are not perfect, remind your team that each player needs to practice returning all shots, and that moving to the ball is part of the game!

Teach your players that two factors are acting on the ball to pull it down in the court: gravity and spin. When they hit the ball flat, gravity must pull the ball down in the court, and they will have to hit the ball lower over the net as they increase their speed. A better plan would be to hit with topspin, which is created when the swing pattern is low to high. This pattern results in the racket brushing up on the ball and causing it to rotate forward, like a ball rolling to the net. The more topspin a player uses, the faster the ball will curve in the court. The player can then hit the ball hard and with plenty of net clearance if there is enough topspin on the ball.

Basic Stroke Skills

This section outlines the basic strokes that you will teach your players at the youth level. These are broken down into three groups—baseline skills, midcourt skills, and net skills. They are presented in the order in which you should introduce them to your players. Remember, as you learned in chapter 6, strokes should be learned in relationship to court positioning and areas of the court. No stroke should be taught without providing the context of where the player is positioned on the court and the purpose of the shot.

Ready Position for Tennis

The ready position is the starting point for all shots (except the serve, which has its own technique depending on the serve used; see Serve on page 82 for more information). Players need to be in the best possible position to read the types of shots that are coming from their opponents in terms of speed, spin, direction, and trajectory so that they can execute successful returns.

Just before the opponent makes contact, the player should be directly facing the opponent with the feet about shoulder-width apart, weight forward and off the heels, and knees flexed (see figure 7.16). The head should be up, the back straight, and the eyes focused on the ball. The racket should be held with the forehand grip, and the weight of the racket should be carried by the nondominant hand. Note that players at the net using a continental grip should hold the racket higher, about head-level height.

Figure 7.16 Ready position for tennis.

Baseline Skills

Strokes hit from the baseline are the foundation for the game of tennis because all points begin with both players at the baseline. These include the first stroke used for every point, which is the serve, followed by forehand and backhand ground strokes, lobs, and service returns.

Serve

The serve is an important offensive stroke used to start every point. Youth players put the ball in play using an overhand serve from the baseline into the service court. (The USTA Jr. Team Tennis' QuickStart format allows the 8 and under age group to use an underhand serve to put the ball in play.)

To execute the full-swing overhand serve, the player stands behind the baseline and sideways to the net, holding the racket with the dominant hand in an eastern forehand grip or a continental grip for more power and spin (see figure 7.17*a*). The player's feet are shoulder-width apart with the front foot at about a 45-degree angle to the net pointing at the net post and the back foot parallel with the baseline. The racket should point toward the service court. The nondominant hand holds the ball lightly in the fingers and supports the weight of the racket. The body should be relaxed. This starting position should be consistent before each serve.

> **Coaching Tip**
> Urge players to develop a preserve ritual to help them relax and focus. This will establish a comfortable routine before each serve and will prevent them from rushing. Adjusting the strings, bouncing the ball, taking a deep breath, and shaking out the hand are all rituals that players use.

From the starting position, the racket arm swings back to shoulder level so the arm is in a full extension and the racket points to the back, with the palm down and knuckles facing up (see figure 7.17*b*). The player's body should be coiled—that is, turned away from the net with the weight on the back foot (the player may also choose a variation of this backswing, in which the upper body simply rotates and the racket swings around at about shoulder height). Once the arm is back and the body is coiled and loaded on the back foot, the knees flex so they can drive up and forward on contact. The hitting arm bends to a 90-degree angle, and the elbow drives up and forward as the body rotates toward the net and the racket head loops behind the back and whips up to the contact point (see figure 7.17*c*). During the elbow bend, the tossing arm reaches up as high as possible and releases the ball into the ideal contact point, which is as high as the racket can reach, in front of the baseline and even with the hitting shoulder. At contact, the racket head reaches maximum acceleration, and the wrist is relaxed so it can snap up and out (see figure 7.17*d*). The tossing arm drops close to the body so the body can rotate forward. The head is up and steady with the eyes on the ball at contact.

Figure 7.17 Full-swing overhand serve.

After the hit, the player's weight continues to move forward, and the back foot steps over the baseline for balance. Some players leave the ground as they drive up and land on the forward foot before the back foot steps forward for balance. The racket follows through across the body and finishes with the hitting hand beside the opposite hip (see figure 7.17*e*). At this time, the server must be ready to react to the return and be able to move right, left, forward, or back.

Slice Serve

The slice serve, an excellent second serve option, is a serve in which a type of spin is imparted to the ball. This allows a player to hit with greater net clearance, yet have the ball curve into the court. To understand a slice serve, first imagine there is a face painted on the ball. A flat serve is one in which the racket hits the "face" on the nose. A slice serve is performed by brushing over the "ear" of the ball. A player must use the continental grip, as shown previously in figure 7.3 on page 70, and must aim much higher than on a flat serve, hitting up and across the ball. If the spin causes the serve to veer too far to the left or right, the player will need to adjust the target to account for the spin.

Serving Drill

To have players practice the serve, set up the court so there are three targets (e.g., cones) in the deuce court and three targets in the ad court. These targets are placed close to the service line and in the outside corners close to the alley to force the opponent out wide, in the middle of the service court directly at the opponent's body to crowd the player, and close to the center service line where the ball goes over the lowest part of the net and can be hit the hardest. A player positioned at the baseline hits a first and second serve to one of the target areas. After the player hits the two serves, he should move to the other side just as he would do when playing a match and hit two more serves to the target areas. Teams of four to six can practice serving at the same time on one court.

Forehand Ground Stroke

The forehand ground stroke is a neutral or defensive stroke used on the dominant side of the body after the ball bounces. Players at the baseline will hit most shots with a ground stroke, either forehand or backhand (as discussed in the next section beginning on page 87), depending on which hand is dominant and whether the ball is hit to the right or left side of the body.

When preparing to hit a forehand ground stroke, the player will assume a ready position just behind the baseline and midway between the sidelines at the center mark. The ready position is a balanced body position in which the feet are about shoulder-width apart with the knees flexed and the back straight (see figure 7.18*a*). The player's weight is forward with the feet and body facing toward the opponent, and the player's eyes are fixed on the ball. The racket should be held loosely between the waist and shoulders using whatever forehand grip the player prefers (eastern, semi-western, or western as described on pages 70-72). The weight of the racket should be supported in the nondominant hand, which is positioned near the throat of the racket.

> **Coaching Tip**
> Younger or less-skilled players may have a tendency to mistime or overhit shots. Players who prepare their rackets late or have backswings that are too long have difficulty making contact with the ball at a contact point that is even with the front foot. If your players have difficulty with timing or power on the hit, have them shorten their backswings to reduce the time it takes for the stroke and to make it much easier to contact the ball even with the front foot. The shorter backswing also reduces the power of the swing so they have more control.

Once the opponent strikes the ball and the player determines the direction of the shot, the player initiates a unit turn in which she releases the racket with the nondominant hand and her body, racket, and feet all turn sideways to the net at the same time and face the forehand side (see figure 7.18*b*). After the turn, the player should move immediately to the contact point where the ball will be hit (see figure 7.18*c*). Ideally, the player will be in good position before the ball lands on the court and will have time to take a few quick, short adjustment steps if necessary. When the player is moving into a position to hit the ball, the racket should be taken back so it points to the back and is below the contact point, allowing it to move forward in a low-to-high swing pattern. The player's weight should be loaded on the back foot.

The forward motion then begins with a step toward the net with the front foot, transferring the weight from the back to the front foot (see figure 7.18*d*). At the same time, the racket swings from below the contact point to the contact point, which is in front of the forward foot and waist high. The hitting arm is fully extended, and the body remains facing sideways on contact.

The racket moves forward through the contact point. For maximum control and power, the player must keep the racket face and swing in line with the target as the racket accelerates through the ball. The hand, arm, and racket will follow through across the body as the hips stop with the body facing the net (see figure 7.18*e*). The racket will continue to follow through and finish up and over the opposite shoulder.

Figure 7.18 Forehand ground stroke.

Forehand Ground Stroke Drill

To have your players practice forehand ground strokes, divide them into pairs and start both players on opposite service lines. One player begins the drill by hitting a foam ball over the net. The players hit forehand crosscourt ground strokes back and forth over the net. When the players have hit 30 consecutive strokes, they move back to a position between the service line and baseline and hit 30 consecutive crosscourt forehand ground strokes using low-compression balls. When they have hit 30 consecutive strokes with the low-compression balls, they move back to the baseline for 30 consecutive crosscourt forehand ground strokes using regular tennis balls. When the players have hit 30 consecutive strokes with tennis balls, they remain at the baseline for 30 consecutive crosscourt forehand ground strokes deep in the court using regular tennis balls.

Backhand Ground Stroke

The backhand ground stroke is a neutral or defensive stroke used on the non-racket side of the body after the ball bounces. As mentioned previously in the forehand ground stroke section, players at the baseline will hit most shots with ground strokes, either backhand or forehand, depending on whether the ball is hit to the right or left side of the body. Players can execute the backhand ground stroke using either one hand or two.

Two-Handed Backhand Ground Stroke When preparing to hit a two-handed backhand ground stroke, the player assumes a ready position just behind the baseline at the center mark (see figure 7.19*a*). The ready position is a balanced body position in which the feet are about shoulder-width apart with the knees flexed and the back straight. The player's weight is forward with the feet and body facing toward the opponent, and the player's eyes are fixed on the ball. The racket should be held loosely between the waist and shoulders. Both hands are held close together on the grip of the racket with the top hand (the nondominant hand) in a semi-western grip position and the bottom hand (the dominant hand) in a continental grip.

Once the opponent strikes the ball and the player determines the direction of the shot, she initiates a unit turn in which her body, racket, and feet all turn sideways to the net at the same time to face the backhand side (see figure 7.19*b*). After the turn, the player should move immediately to the contact point where the ball will be hit. Ideally, the player will be in a good position before the ball lands on the court and will have time to take a few quick, short adjustment steps if necessary. When moving into a position to hit the ball, the player should take the racket back so it points to the back fence and is below the contact

Figure 7.19 Two-handed backhand ground stroke.

point, allowing it to move forward in a low-to-high swing pattern (see figure 7.19*c*). The player's weight should be loaded on the back foot.

The player's forward motion begins with a step toward the net with the front foot, transferring the weight from the back to the front foot and turning the hips and shoulders so that the body faces the net (see figure 7.19*d*). At the same time, the racket accelerates through the contact point, which is waist high and even with the front foot (see figure 7.19*e*). The arms are slightly bent at the elbows. The nondominant top hand will be on the same plane as the racket face and should be directed at the target on the opponent's side of the net. At contact, the racket face and top hand extend through the contact point, and the racket follows through over the opposite shoulder. As the stroke ends, the body weight shifts to the forward foot.

One-Handed Backhand Ground Stroke When preparing to hit a one-handed backhand ground stroke, the player assumes a ready position just behind the baseline at the center mark. The ready position is a balanced body position in which the feet are about shoulder-width apart with the knees flexed and the back straight (see figure 7.20*a*). The player's weight is forward with the feet and body facing toward the opponent, and the player's eyes are fixed on the ball. The racket should be held loosely between the waist and shoulders using whatever forehand grip the player prefers (eastern, semi-western, or western as described on pages 70-72). The weight of the racket should be supported in the nondominant hand, which is positioned near the throat of the racket.

Once the opponent strikes the ball and the player determines the direction of the shot, the player initiates a unit turn in which he takes the racket back with his nondominant hand and his body, racket, and feet all turn sideways to the net at the same time to face the backhand side (see figure 7.20*b*). During the unit turn, the player changes from the forehand grip to the eastern backhand grip. After the turn, the player should move immediately to the contact point where the ball will be hit. Ideally, the player will be in a good position before the ball lands on the court and will have time to take a few quick, short adjustment steps if necessary. When moving into a position to hit the ball, the player should take the racket back so it points to the back fence and below the contact point, allowing it to move forward in a low-to-high swing pattern (see figure 7.20*c*). The player's weight should be loaded on the back foot.

The forward motion begins with a step toward the net with the front foot, transferring the player's weight from the back to the front foot. The nondominant hand releases the racket and stays back during the forward weight transfer and swing. This will prevent the hips and shoulders from turning so they face the net. The power in a one-handed backhand comes from the legs and the weight transfer from the back foot to the forward foot (see figure 7.20*d*). At the same time, the racket swings from below the contact point to the contact point, which is in front of the forward foot and waist high. The hitting arm is fully extended and straight. The nondominant arm stays back, and the body remains facing sideways at the hit. At contact, for a topspin backhand, the racket face points to the target and the arm and racket move through the ball and finish high so the hand is at head level and the racket is pointing at the sky (see figure 7.20*e*). Note that for a backspin backhand, the racket begins above the contact point and swings in a high-to-level pattern with the racket face slightly open at the contact point.

Figure 7.20 One-handed backhand ground stroke.

Backhand Ground Stroke Drill

To have your players practice backhand ground strokes, divide them into groups of four, with two players positioned at each service line. To begin the drill, one player from one of the groups drop feeds a foam ball over the net using a backhand ground stroke and immediately moves out of the way so that a partner can be ready to hit the return shot. One of the players on the opposite line returns the ball using a backhand ground stroke and also moves out of the way so that a partner can then be ready to return the ball when it comes back. Players continue to alternate and hit crosscourt backhand ground strokes until they have made 20 consecutive hits. At that point they move back to a position between the service line and baseline and hit until they have hit 20 consecutive crosscourt backhand ground strokes using low-compression balls. At that point they move back to the baseline for 20 consecutive crosscourt backhand ground strokes using regular tennis balls.

Lob

A lob is a shot that travels high over the net, bounces in the opponent's court, and travels over the opposite baseline. It can be a defensive shot when a player is pulled out of the court or is well behind the baseline and the opponent is in an offensive net position. The defensive lob serves two purposes: It gives a player time to recover to a better position on the court, and it forces the opponent away from the net to play a less offensive shot. The lob can also be played as a more offensive shot when a player is on or behind the baseline but has time to get set.

When preparing to hit a lob, the player assumes a ready position behind the center mark (see figure 7.21*a*). The ready position is a balanced body position in which the feet are about shoulder-width apart with the knees flexed and the back straight. The player's weight is forward with the feet and body facing toward the opponent, and the player's eyes are fixed on the ball. The racket should be held loosely between the waist and shoulders using a forehand grip. The weight of the racket should be supported in the nondominant hand, which is positioned near the throat of the racket.

Once the opponent strikes the ball and the player determines the direction of the shot, the player initiates a unit turn in which he releases the racket with his nondominant hand and his body, racket, and feet all turn sideways to the net at the same time to face the forehand or backhand side (see figure 7.21*b* for an example of a unit turn to the forehand side). After the turn, the player should move immediately to the contact point where the ball will be hit. Ideally, the player will be in a good position before the ball lands on the court and will have time to take a few quick, short adjustment steps if necessary. While moving into position to hit the ball, the player should take the racket back so it points to the back and below the contact point, allowing it to move in a low-to-high swing pattern. The player's weight should be loaded on the back foot.

The forward motion then begins with a step toward the net with the front foot, transferring the player's weight from the back to the front foot (see figure 7.21*c*). At the same time, the racket swings from below the contact point to the contact point, which is in front of the forward foot and about head height, with the hitting arm fully extended. The nondominant arm stays back, and the body remains facing sideways on contact (see figure 7.21*d*). For the lob, the racket face will be open at the contact point to make the ball travel up off the strings. The open racket face will cause the ball to go up (see figure 7.21*e*), with the apex of the lob ideally aligning over the net. The racket will finish over the head with the hand at about eye height (see figure 7.21*f*).

Ideally, the player will set and load on the back foot so he can drive forward and rotate his body toward the net. This is often not possible because he is on the move even at the point of contact. If this is the case, the player must still swing from low to high and make contact with an open racket face to get the ball up and over the opponent. The farther the player is from the center mark, the higher he should hit the lob to create more time to recover into a better court position. Even if the lob is short, the opponent will not have an easy shot if the player at the baseline can return to a good ready position behind the center mark and be ready for the shot.

Figure 7.21 Lob.

Lob Drill

To have your players practice the lob, divide them into pairs with one player in a ready position behind the baseline and the center mark and an opponent in the ready position for the volley in the opposite court halfway between the service line and the net. Position yourself by the net on the opponent's side of the net and feed a ball to one of the deep corners of the court. The player at the baseline must run wide to get to the ball, hit a high lob over the opponent at the net, and be back in a ready position behind the baseline and the center mark by the time the ball lands on the court. As soon as the ball hits the court, feed a second ball to either deep corner so the player must move, set up, lob, and recover as described previously. Feed a series of four balls before rotating the players.

As a variation, give the player at the net the opportunity to hit an overhead smash if the ball would land in the service court and then have both players play out the point. After the point, both players move back to the positions they were in when starting the drill. Feed the next ball until all four feeds are completed.

d

e

f

Service Return

The service return is the second-most-played shot in the game, next to the actual serve. A player who develops a consistent and dependable service return puts tremendous pressure on the server to hit strong and accurate serves.

Before the opponent begins the service motion, the receiver assumes a ready position at the baseline, halfway between the two service lines (see figure 7.22*a*). For powerful servers, receivers should move back a step or two behind the baseline to give themselves more time to turn, move to the ball, prepare, and make the return. Conversely, with weaker servers, the receivers should start inside the baseline. The ready position is a balanced body position in which the feet are about shoulder-width apart with the knees flexed and the back straight. The player's weight is forward with the feet and body facing toward the server, and the player's eyes are fixed on the server's contact point. The racket should be held loosely between the waist and shoulders using a forehand grip. The weight of the racket should be supported in the nondominant hand, which is positioned near the throat of the racket. Many players hop forward into a split step position just before making contact so they can land with their weight forward and react, either right or left, to the serve (see figure 7.22*b*).

a b c

Figure 7.22 Service return.

Once the server strikes the ball and the player determines the direction of the shot, he initiates a unit turn in which his body, racket, and feet all turn sideways to the net at the same time to face the forehand or backhand side (see figure 7.22*c* for an example of a unit turn to the backhand side). After the turn, the player should move immediately to the contact point where the ball will be hit (see figure 7.22*d*). The difference between the service return and other strokes is that the player will have much less time to move to the ball for a return. Typically it can end up being just one quick step. While moving into position to hit the ball, the player should take the racket back for a short and compact backswing. The player's weight should be loaded on the back foot.

From this point, the weight shifts forward and the body turns and faces the net (see figure 7.22*e*). The racket swings with a slight low-to-high swing pattern and makes contact even with the front hip and at waist height with the elbows slightly bent. The racket face drives through the contact point and finishes over the opposite shoulder (see figure 7.22*f*). The racket must be held firmly at contact because of the force of the serve. After the return, the receiver should recover to behind the center mark behind the baseline.

Service Return Drill

To have your players practice the service return, divide them into pairs and start each player on opposite service lines. One player is the server and begins the drill by hitting serves to the other player, the service receiver. Positioning players on the service line, rather than the baseline, which is the normal serving position, will cause the balls to get to the service receiver quickly, and the server will make far fewer errors getting the ball into the service court. This will maximize the service receiver's chances of hitting returns successfully. Players switch places after two minutes of play.

Midcourt Skills

Midcourt skills are shots inside the baseline and are often used to set up the next shot by allowing the player to move into a more favorable offensive position at the net. Midcourt skills include the approach shot, the drop shot, and the sharp-angled crosscourt shot.

All midcourt skills can be hit on either the forehand or backhand side. Begin teaching midcourt skills to your players by teaching them how to play these from the forehand side. Once they have learned this, they can then learn how to perform them from the backhand side, using either one or two hands.

Approach Shot

An approach shot is hit while a player is moving forward to the net in order give himself time to get into a more offensive net position for the next hit. When your player hits an approach shot, it should land deep in the opponent's court so he will have time to get to the net and the opponent will be forced to play his next shot from well behind the baseline. The approach shot can also be used to return weak second serves. Power is not essential for this shot because the main purpose is to get into a net position for the next shot. The harder the player hits the ball, the quicker it will be, and the less time he will have to move into that net position.

Approach shots are typically hit from short balls, so the player should assume the same ready position at the baseline as he would for either forehand or backhand ground strokes, as discussed on pages 81 through 91. A player should anticipate a short ball when his opponent is forced out of position or is attempting a hit before he is fully prepared and set. As soon as a player sees that the ball will land short in the court and inside the service line, he should move forward and make a unit turn sideways to the net just prior to the stroke so he can make contact at the highest point after the bounce (see figure 7.23 for an example of the approach shot on the forehand side).

Because power is not essential, the player is moving forward, and the distance the ball must travel to reach the baseline is less, the backswing used for

a b c

Figure 7.23 Forehand approach shot.

the approach shot is shorter than the backswing used for a ground stroke hit from baseline to baseline. There are two swing patterns for approach shots—a high-to-level swing pattern that creates backspin on the ball and a low-to-high swing pattern that creates topspin on the ball.

High-to-Level Swing Pattern A high-to-level swing pattern that creates backspin on the ball requires that the racket face be slightly open at contact. The ball will be hit with a low trajectory and will land deep in the court near the baseline on the opponent's side of the court. Because the ball is hit low and with backspin, it will skid on the court and stay low, causing the opponent to get low and hit up on the ball to get it over the net. The other player, who is now at a position at the net, will have an easy ball to hit using a volley or overhead.

The advantage of the backspin approach shot is that it can be hit softer for control, yet it will travel deep in the court. The ball will stay low and force the opponent to hit his next shot up. Because the ball is not hit as hard, it gives the player more time to move to the net and be set in a good volley position. If the backspin shot is hit too high, however, it will either float over the baseline or land in the court where the opponent will have plenty of time to set up and drive a return. Some players with excellent topspin ground strokes have difficulty changing to the swing pattern necessary for backspin shots, so they tend to make unforced errors when hitting with backspin.

Low-to-High Swing Pattern A low-to-high swing pattern that creates topspin on the ball requires that the swing be much flatter than that of a topspin ground stroke. This low-to-high swing will provide some topspin but not the excessive spin that would cause a high arching or looping shot. The topspin will enable the player to hit a firm shot deep in the court without the ball sailing over the baseline. A player should move forward after playing this more aggressive and forcing approach shot so she is in a good position at the net for the opponent's weak return.

The advantage of the topspin approach shot is that it can be hit hard and close to the baseline, giving the opponent very little time to set up for the return. However, because the ball is hit hard, the player hitting the approach shot has much less time to move to the net and be set up in a good volley position.

Approach Shot Drill

Position all players in a single-file line behind the baseline and stand in the alley just inside the service line. To begin, gently toss a ball underhand to the first player in line so that it lands inside the service line. The player hits the ball using an approach shot and moves forward to assume a ready position at the net as though preparing for a volley, before the ball bounces in the court on the opposite side of the net. The deeper the player hits the approach shot and the quicker the player can move to the net, the better chance she will have of being set by the time the ball lands. The player moves to the end of the line after one shot, and the drill is repeated with the next player in line.

Drop Shot

A drop shot is hit from inside the baseline so the ball just clears the net and lands softly on the court. The perfect drop shot bounces twice before the opponent can move forward to hit the return. However, even if the opponent reaches and returns the ball before the second bounce, he will have to hit the ball up softly while on the run, and his position will be close to the net. It is quite easy for the other player to then exploit the opponent's soft return and close net position with a lob hit into the backcourt.

Drop shots are played from the same ready position as all other strokes hit from the baseline (such as the forehand and backhand ground strokes discussed on pages 81-91 and the approach shots discussed on pages 96-98). The drop shot should be used only when a player can move forward inside the baseline and the opponent is behind the baseline or is either slow or tired (see figure 7.24 for an example of a drop shot from the forehand side).

Because the ball does not travel very far both before and after the bounce, the drop shot is hit with a very short backswing and with backspin so the ball

Figure 7.24 Forehand drop shot.

does not hit and bounce forward. The racket moves in a high-to-level swing pattern, and the racket face is open at the contact point. The grip is soft and relaxed to absorb the shock of the ball hitting the strings.

After hitting the drop shot, the player should recover to the baseline and be ready for the opponent's return. Assuming the shot is returned by the opponent, the player should then be able to hit a lob over the opponent's head or a ground stroke to either side of the opponent.

Drop Shot Drill

To have your players practice the drop shot, divide them into pairs and start one player (A) between the service line and the net and the other player (B) at the service line. Player A drop feeds a drop shot so it lands just over the net and runs back to touch the service line before she can play the next shot. Player B moves forward to return the ball using a drop shot and runs back to touch the service line before playing the next shot. Players continue to alternate between hitting a drop shot, running back to touch the service line, and moving forward to play another drop shot before the ball bounces twice on the court. If the ball bounces twice on the court, two new players rotate in and repeat the drill.

Sharp-Angled Crosscourt Shot

A sharp-angled crosscourt shot is a ball that is hit on such an angle that it lands near the intersection of the service line and the sideline. To hit the ball with enough angle to make this possible, a player must hit the shot from inside the baseline, the closer to the net the better, and the ball must be away from the center of the court. The closer to the sideline the shot is hit, the more angle is possible. A sharp-angled crosscourt shot is used to hit outright winners or to pull an opponent out of the court to create openings for the next shot.

A sharp-angled crosscourt shot is hit from the same ready position as all other strokes hit from the baseline (such as the forehand and backhand ground strokes discussed on pages 81-91 and the approach shots discussed on pages 96-98). However, for the crosscourt shot, the player must move inside the baseline to be able to hit with enough angle for the shot to be effective. The player should hit the shot with topspin because the ball must clear the net and drop quickly in the court. To hit with enough topspin, the player should use a short low-to-high swing path pattern, as shown for the forehand in figure 7.25. The racket will start at least a foot below the contact point and finish with the hand over the opposite shoulder at head level. Because the ball does not have a great deal of distance to travel before it would fly over the sideline, hitting with the right speed and spin is essential. Direction, not speed, is most important for a sharp-angled shot, and topspin will pull the ball into the court. After hitting the crosscourt shot, the player should then quickly recover back so he is ready if the opponent returns the ball.

a b c

Figure 7.25 Forehand sharp-angled crosscourt shot.

Sharp-Angled Crosscourt Shot Drill

Position all players in a single-file line behind the baseline and stand in the court on the opposite side of the net. To begin, feed a short, wide ball into the court to the first player in line. The player moves in, hits a sharp-angled crosscourt shot, and quickly recovers back to the baseline. Feed a second ball back into the court on whichever side you choose, to the same player, who must move, set up, and hit the second shot back into the opening on the opposite side of the court. The player rotates to the end of the line after two shots, and the drill is repeated with the next player in line.

Net Skills

A player in a good ready position halfway between the service line and the net has a tremendous position advantage. Being close to the net gives the player a much wider angle to use when hitting balls away from the opponent. The player at the net can hit the ball hard and into the openings on the court when the contact point is above the top of the net. This good net position gives the opponent much less time to react to and prepare for the shot hit by the player at the net and also forces the opponent to attempt higher-risk shots by aiming returns closer to the lines and lower over the net. Net skills used at the youth level include the volley and the overhead smash.

Volley

When positioned at the net, players use volleys to hit the ball before it bounces with the intent to end the point by angling the ball away from the opponent or hitting the ball sharply into and through the court.

Approach Volley

Approach volleys are shots hit in the air, before the ball bounces, inside the baseline while a player is moving forward. This shot is played when the opponent hits a high looping shot that would bounce deep in the court close to the baseline. To hit this shot, the player moves quickly forward and takes a full swing similar to that for a ground stroke, hitting the ball before it bounces. After hitting the approach volley, the player should move quickly to the net so he can volley the weak return into the open court.

The advantage of hitting an approach volley is that it gives an opponent much less time to prepare for the next shot. The player's position is greatly improved because he is moving forward to get the ball out of the air and well into the court rather than backing up and playing a high bouncing ball behind the baseline. This puts pressure on the opponent and takes away the option of just hitting safe, high, floating returns when he is in trouble.

To have players practice the approach volley, start them at the baseline and feed a soft, high shot toward the backcourt. Players should move forward so they hit the ball out of the air at waist level or above. They should move through the ball at contact and to the net so they are in a volley position midway between the service line and the net by the time the ball lands on the opponent's side of the court.

When preparing to volley, the player assumes a ready position between the service line and the net (see figure 7.26). Positioning closer to the net is advantageous because it increases the angles available for the volley (note, however, that this position is vulnerable to the lob). If a player is positioned closer to the service line, the ball is most likely hit from below the top of the net, thus causing the volley to be hit up in order to get it over the net. In addition, a ball hit from a position close to the service line cannot be hit hard because the ball is generally contacted below the top of the net and the player must hit up on the ball. The ready position is a balanced body position in which the feet are about shoulder-width apart with the knees flexed and the back straight. The player's weight is forward with the feet and body facing toward the opponent, and the player's eyes are on the opponent and the ball. The racket should be held with the head of the racket about shoulder level, which is slightly higher than the ground stroke ready position at the baseline. The reason is that this is generally the height of the ball at contact. The player grips the racket loosely in a continental grip with the weight of the racket supported by the nondominant hand, which is positioned near the throat of the racket. The continental grip is ideal because it can be used for both forehands and backhands without a grip change and naturally positions the racket face slightly open at the contact point on both the forehand and backhand sides.

Figure 7.26 Ready position for the volley.

For a picture-perfect volley, once the opponent has struck the ball and the player determines the direction of the shot, the player initiates a unit turn in which she releases the racket with her nondominant hand, and her body, racket, and feet all turn sideways to the net at the same time to face either the forehand or backhand side (see figure 7.27). At the same time, the player positions the face of the racket behind the ball. The speed of the oncoming ball will determine the amount of backswing that is possible. If the oncoming ball is fast, there will be little or no time for a backswing, and the volley is hit by blocking the ball back in the court. If a player has additional time, she can add a short backswing for extra power on the volley (these two scenarios are

Figure 7.27 Unit turn for the volley.

discussed later in this section). After the turn, the player should move immediately to the contact point where the ball will be hit. Ideally, the player will then be in good position and still have time to take a few quick, short adjustment steps if necessary. The player's weight should be loaded on the back foot.

The forward motion then begins with a step forward and across the body, transferring the player's weight from the back to the front foot. At the same time, the player hits the ball at a contact point even with the front hip and with the head of the racket above the wrist. The swing pattern is level when the contact point is above the net (see figure 7.28, *a-c*). For lower balls, the player must use a slight low-to-high pattern (see figure 7.29, *a-c*) and must hit the ball with an upward trajectory and softly so it doesn't fly out of the court. Soft, sharp-angled volleys are played with a soft and relaxed grip to absorb the shock at contact. The follow-through ends shortly after the contact point, with the racket moving forward and through the ball and ending with the racket face still directed at the target. The follow-through could be slightly longer if the player has time for a slightly longer backswing for extra power.

As mentioned previously, a player facing a fast-approaching ball may not have time to set up for a picture-perfect volley. He may only have time to block the ball back into the court, as shown in figure 7.30. In this case, the player will prepare for contact by simply squaring the racket face behind the ball on either the forehand or backhand side. Have the player imagine he is holding a hand mirror and wants to position the mirror (racket face) so the ball could see itself in the mirror. The player then holds the grip firmly and blocks the ball with no further backswing or follow-through so that it goes back into the opponent's open court.

a

b

c

Figure 7.28 Swing pattern for a volley when the contact point is above the net.

Figure 7.29 Swing pattern for a volley when the contact point is below the top of the net.

Sometimes a player may have a little more time before hitting the volley, but not as much as she would for a picture-perfect volley. In this case, the player can take a step forward at the hit to generate more power, as shown in figure 7.31. When she turns her body to the side on the unit turn, her hips and shoulders will face the sideline and her weight will be on her back foot. At this point, she can step forward to contact the ball even with the front hip. Contact with the ball can occur any time during this sequence depending on the speed of the opponent's shot.

Figure 7.30 Hitting a volley by blocking the ball back into the opponent's court.

a b c

Figure 7.31 Stepping forward when hitting a volley to generate more power.

For broader net coverage, rather than using a unit turn, a player can use a crossover step toward the net to hit a volley. This would be used when the ball is hit away from the player at the net where she would have to move wide to get to the ball. The crossover step is both forward and toward the sideline at about a 45-degree angle to the net and will cause the weight to shift forward from the back foot to the front foot (see figure 7.32, *a-c*). By moving at a 45-degree angle to the net, players can cut off opponents' passing shots. Again, contact with the ball can occur any time during this sequence depending on the speed of the opponent's shot.

Volley Drill

To have your players practice volleys, divide them into pairs and start both players on opposite sides of the net, halfway between the net and service lines. To begin, using a foam ball, one player puts the ball into play using a self-feed or an underhand toss and players volley back and forth, keeping the ball in the air and hitting both forehand and backhand volleys as necessary. Because a foam ball moves more slowly than a tennis ball, players will have more time to turn, prepare the racket, and step forward for each volley and to hop back into a good ready position after hitting each volley. After 30 consecutive volleys with the foam ball, players can then progress to 20 consecutive volleys using low-compression balls and ultimately end with 20 consecutive volleys using regular tennis balls.

a b c

Figure 7.32 Using the crossover step for broader net coverage when hitting a volley.

Overhead Smash

The overhead smash is a shot hit close to the net with an overhand motion, much like a serve. It is used to return a lob. In most situations the overhead smash is hit before the ball bounces on the court, but it can be hit after the bounce if the lob is very high or in the sun, or if the ball is difficult to track because of windy conditions. Players can hit this shot with wide angles away from the opponent. In addition, the ball is played at full arm and racket extension, allowing the player to hit forcefully down into the court. Of all the shots, the overhead smash has the greatest likelihood of winning a point.

When preparing to use an overhead smash, the player assumes a ready position midway between the service line and the net (see figure 7.33*a*). The ready position is a balanced body position in which the feet are about shoulder-width apart with the knees flexed and the back straight. The player's weight is forward with the feet and body facing toward the opponent, and the player's eyes are on the opponent and the ball. The head of the racket should be about shoulder height. Note that this is slightly higher than the ground stroke ready position at the baseline. The player grips the racket loosely in a continental grip with the weight of the racket supported by the nondominant hand, which is positioned near the throat of the racket. The continental grip is ideal because it can be used for both forehand and backhand volleys or overhead smashes without a grip change.

As soon as the ball leaves the opponent's racket and the player realizes the opponent's return is a lob, the player can adjust his position as necessary. For example, positioning closer to the net is advantageous because it increases the angles available for the overhead. When players are deeper in the court (at or behind the service line), overhead shots should be hit to the corners of the opponent's court rather than angled over the sidelines. The player then initiates a quick unit turn in which his body, racket, and feet all turn sideways to the net at the same time to face the forehand side for an overhead (see figure 7.33*b*).

At the same time, the arm is pulled back about shoulder height, and the elbow is bent in a throwing position, as though the player were getting into a serving position by simply turning the body and preparing the racket to throw. The nondominant hand will be forward for balance. From this position, the player must then move into a position in which he can contact the ball over his right shoulder, as high as he can reach with his arm and racket. The player adjusts his footwork depending on where the lob will land. This might consist of a few quick adjustment steps for easy lobs or four or five crossover steps away from the net to retrieve deep lobs when the player is facing the sideline. An important tip for your players to remember is that for the smash, the unit turn to the side and racket preparation must be completed before the player moves to the position in which he will hit the ball so that the movement occurs with the player facing the sideline. If he does not turn, he will be facing the net and will have very limited movement away from the net as he backpedals with the weight on his heels.

Once the player is in position to hit the lob, his head and eyes should be up and his weight should be on the back foot (see figure 7.33*c*). The forward swing begins with the weight shifting forward and the body rotating so the hips and shoulders face the net. The arm swings up and forward, leading with the elbow, and the racket makes contact with a relaxed wrist snap and maximum racket speed at contact (see figure 7.33*d*). The follow-through will be across the body so the hitting hand finishes outside the opposite hip. Immediately after hitting the overhead smash, the player should move into the ready position at the net in preparation for a volley or another overhead smash if the opponent returns the ball. If the lob is hit very high, if the ball is in the sun, or if there are windy conditions, players might elect to let the ball bounce before hitting the overhead. The technique is the same, but the body position will be farther from the net because the ball will bounce and travel deeper in the court.

Figure 7.33 Overhead smash.

Overhead Smash Drill

To have your players practice the overhead smash, divide them into groups of three, with two players at the baseline and one player in a net position on the opposite side of the court. To begin, one of the players at the baseline starts the drill with a lob using a drop feed. The player in the net position hits an overhead smash, and the players at the baseline attempt to return the ball to the net player using a lob. The baseline players try to get every ball back in play using another lob, and the net player hits an overhead smash on every lob over the net. Each baseline player has two balls each. Have players play as many lob–overhead smash sequences as possible before baseline players feed another lob. After all four balls have been used, players rotate positions.

8

Coaching Singles and Doubles Play

Teaching the tactical skills of tennis—the skills of the game in conjunction with the basic technical skills covered in chapter 7—is at the heart of the games approach. This chapter introduces styles of play for singles and formations for doubles play, in addition to covering the most common game situations your players will encounter and the strategies they need to use to be successful.

Singles Play

Simply stated, singles play in tennis is one person against another. Good singles players know their strengths and use them to win more points than their opponents or to force their opponents to make errors. They must know the styles of play that best suit their individual strengths and how these styles relate to game situations and the tactical skills necessary for successful play.

Styles of Play for Singles

Many team sports have various positions, and coaches must determine where each player fits best based on a number of characteristics. For example, basketball teams have guards, forwards, and centers; baseball teams have outfielders, infielders, catchers, and pitchers. Players are matched with specific positions based on attributes such as size, strength, speed, ball-handling skills, and decision-making skills. In tennis, singles players also have specific characteristics that fall into general styles of play.

As a coach, you should help your players determine the styles of play that best suit them based on their skill levels, strength, speed, and temperaments and help them develop the technical and tactical skills that will build on these strengths. The following sections outline the most common styles of play that you will see at the youth level.

Counter-Punch Baseline Player

The counter-punch baseline player is the most conservative of players. A counter-punch baseline player is most comfortable when she and her opponent are both at the baseline hitting ground strokes at a comfortable speed. Such a player is very content in this position because she is not forced to hit defensively, nor is she taking the opportunity to hit more aggressively. This player generally makes the fewest errors because she would rather win points by having her opponent make errors than by hitting winning shots herself.

The counter-punch baseline player is typically in good physical condition and has endurance and speed, a long patience threshold, and good forehand and backhand ground stroke skills. When this player is attacked by an opponent coming to the net, she can accurately hit balls to either side of or over the opponent. The counter-punch baseline player needs to be very consistent and should play with minimal errors. Smaller players or players without specific strengths can be very successful playing this style because they force their opponents to hit high-risk shots that result in more errors. Many times when the counter-puncher returns the ball and the opponent makes errors, the opponent will either hit harder and closer to the lines, thus creating even more errors, or she will fall into the style of the counter-puncher and just get balls back into the court. More aggressive players are easily frustrated with this style of play.

Coaching Tip
Some players are proficient at more than one style of play; such players might need to change from one style to another depending on an opponent or the playing conditions. For example, the counter-punch baseline player could easily be an aggressive baseline player when a strong wind is at her back, or the all-court player could adopt a more attacking style with an opponent who panics and rushes his shots when he has less time to react.

Aggressive Baseline Player

The aggressive baseline player, like the counter-punch baseline player, prefers to stay in the backcourt and hit ground strokes rather than move forward to the net position. The difference between the aggressive baseline player and the counter-punch baseline player is that the aggressive baseline player actively tries to create openings in the opponent's court so he can hit shots with power to end the point. This style carries more risk than the counter-punch because the player hits side-to-side with enough angle and with more speed to create those openings.

The aggressive baseline player has excellent ground stroke skills on both the forehand and backhand side but typically has developed a powerful forehand ground stroke as his weapon. This player will generally hit the forehand ground stroke from inside the baseline and hit hard and away from the opponent. He can often end points with one shot. When the opponent is able to return the ball, he often does so weakly, and the aggressive baseline player is ready to play another hard-hit ground stroke to the other corner of the court to win the point. Because the aggressive baseline player likes to hit the ball hard to create openings in the opponent's court, one of the challenges for this type of player is being consistent and patient long enough to get an easy ball in a good position so he can play it aggressively.

All-Court Player

The all-court player has a great deal of variety in her game. This style takes the longest time to develop because so many skills are necessary. The all-court player is comfortable in every area of the court—at the baseline, midcourt, and at the net—and has a variety of strong shots to match. This player has the ability to create openings by moving the opponent around the court using a variety of angles, spins, and speeds and can construct points by playing to her own strengths and her opponent's weaknesses. This player can take advantage of any shot that the opponent hits and can set up points by playing a number of shots in a specific pattern with the goal of getting into a position on the court to hit a winning shot. For this reason, this player must also have the patience to play several shots before going for a winner.

The all-court player can play defense if necessary and can be ready to move from a neutral or defensive position to a more offensive position by hitting a more aggressive attacking shot if she gets an easy or short ball from her opponent. For example, the all-court player could be playing a defensive shot from well behind the baseline and quickly move forward to play an aggressive, point-ending shot if the opponent hits a short or weak return. In addition, the all-court player is more likely to adapt to other styles depending on the conditions or her opponent because of the wide range of skills in her repertoire.

Attacking Player

The attacking player takes the most risks of all of the styles. Such a player has a strong serve and prefers to get to the net as soon as possible and hit volleys and overheads to end points quickly, rather than stay at the baseline hitting ground strokes. The attacking player forces the opponent to hit quickly because he is constantly moving forward. By playing close to the net, he gives his opponent less time to set up and return shots.

Attacking players are generally tall and strong, but not necessarily fast or in the best condition. These players must master the ability to hit hard, forcing serves and quickly move forward to volley weak returns. They generally become impatient, however, if the points last more than a few hits. They would rather end the point quickly than construct a point with a series of shots.

Game Situations for Singles

In every tennis game, players perform specific functions regardless of their styles of play. Players may handle even these specific functions slightly differently, however, depending on the styles they are playing.

Serving

The serve is the most common shot played in tennis because every point must begin with a serve. Players hit serves with different goals in mind, depending on their styles of play:

- The counter-punch baseline player generally is not very risky with her first serve and just tries to get the ball in play.
- The aggressive baseline player hits a more aggressive first serve. If the return is short and weak, he generally moves inside the baseline to hit his favorite shot, the aggressive forehand or backhand ground stroke.
- The all-court player hits a variety of serves with different speeds, spins, and angles to keep her opponent from getting into a rhythm. She typically

takes advantage of a weak return with an approach shot, an aggressive ground stroke, or even a drop shot from inside the baseline.

- The attacking player hits a powerful first and even second serve. This high-risk serve typically results in an outright winner or a weak return, allowing the server to move forward to the net for a point-ending volley.

Receiving

The second most commonly hit shot in tennis is the return of serve. The receiver must get the ball back into the server's court before any point can be constructed. Players return serves with different goals in mind, depending on their styles of play:

- The counter-punch baseline player is very consistent and conservative; typically, this player just attempts to return every serve to keep the ball in play rather than hit outright winners. This player strives to neutralize the server; therefore, no matter how hard the serve is, she returns it so that the server must play another shot to win the point. Even on a second serve, the counter-puncher will be content to get the ball back in play without taking risks by hitting the ball hard or close to the lines.
- The aggressive baseline player plays a steady, high-percentage return on good first serves, but he tries to hit to one side or the other to get the server moving after the return. He is ready to hit aggressively and possibly even win points on returns hit from weak second serves.
- The all-court player uses a number of shots to return the serve. She may block powerful serves back into the court or step forward and play more aggressively when she has the opportunity. She can hit approach shots or sharp-angled returns on weak second serves.
- The attacking player tries to use the speed of the first serve and drive it back at the server to take control of the point. He tries to hit returns and get to the net whenever possible to be in a position to win points with a volley or overhead. On second serves he may step forward and play even more aggressively.

Rallying

A rally is a neutral position in which both players are at the baseline and neither has the advantage. The rally is where most points begin to develop and is the start of one player taking control of the point. Players rally with different goals in mind, depending on their styles of play:

- The counter-punch baseline player is very content in the rally position and tries to maintain this position on both sides of the court. If the counter-punch baseline player keeps the opponent deep and she cannot attack, the counter-puncher forces her to hit many shots in the hope that she will make an unforced error.

- The aggressive baseline player is comfortable with the rally position, but he tries to move the opponent from side to side to set up a shot in which he can move inside the baseline to hit hard.
- The all-court player is also comfortable in the neutral rallying position, but she moves an opponent side to side or up and back by hitting at different angles, speeds, spins, and depths if possible.
- The attacking player spends very little time in the neutral rallying position. He might hit one or two balls before going on the attack and rushing the net to end the point.

Playing Offense

When a player is close to the net, she can play offensively by hitting shots that will either end the point or force a weak return from her opponent. Volleys and overheads are considered offensive shots, and ground strokes played from a position inside the baseline are also more likely to be offensive, especially if the opponent is out of an ideal court position. Players play offense with different goals in mind, depending on their styles of play:

- The counter-punch baseline player is not looking to play offensively and will probably take these opportunities to attack to get the ball back and return to a neutral position.
- The aggressive baseline player plays attacking ground strokes when he has the opportunity to hit from inside the baseline. His goal is to hit all of his shots from the backcourt, and he is content to play aggressive baseline shots until he ends the point.
- The all-court player takes advantage of an offensive position when she gets a short or weak return by hitting an aggressive ground stroke or an approach shot and then moving to the net position. Because she is comfortable at either the baseline or the net, she takes opportunities to get to the net whenever possible because it is easier to win points with a volley or overhead.
- The attacking player takes every opportunity to hit shots and move into a more offensive position because playing offense is what he enjoys most. He takes advantage of any opportunity to move closer to the net on any ball so he can be in his most comfortable position.

Playing Defense

When opponents are hitting aggressive shots or are in ideal positions at the net, your players will have no option but to play defensively. Players play defensively with different goals in mind, depending on their styles of play:

- The counter punch-baseline player plays defense well and actually prefers to play defense over offense. She is comfortable getting balls back and forcing her opponent to hit winners.

- The aggressive baseline player is also comfortable playing defense because of his strength from the backcourt. He can adjust from this defensive position and hit more aggressive ground strokes if he gets a short ball in return.
- The all-court player can play defensive shots and takes advantage of any weak shot to be more offensive. The all-court player attempts to hit defensive shots, such as lobs, over the opponent's head on the weaker side, or with topspin so the ball lands on the court and bounces toward the back fence.
- The attacking player is not comfortable playing defense. He doesn't like to be in the backcourt when the opponent is at the net, and he doesn't like to hit lobs or high ground strokes when he is out of position, which is exactly what he must learn to do until he has a better opportunity.

Tactics for Singles Play

Young players learn how to play points effectively by learning the basic tactics used by all singles players regardless of their styles of play. The following four tactics, beginning with the most basic, provide a road map for any player wanting to develop a game plan for playing any opponent. These tactics apply to all levels of play, and more advanced players will use all of these in combination during a match.

Keeping the Ball in Play

Tennis is a game of errors. Players can win matches only if they get more balls back in the court than their opponents, or make fewer errors than their opponents. Young players can be successful by simply keeping the ball in play. Tennis players in the younger age groups who can keep the ball in play will beat many of their opponents. At more advanced levels, however, players have to do more to win matches, such as hitting from side to side to create openings or directing shots to opponents' weaker sides. Note that this is generally the first tactic young tennis players learn and is the one mastered in the counter-punch style.

Hitting to the Open Court

Simply hitting balls deep in the court is a good tactic for young players, but it does not typically require opponents to move, get them tired, or move them out of position. Rather, your players' ability to hit side to side and up and back will force their opponents to move and play shots out of their comfort zones, as well as create openings in the court.

Novice tennis players often just exchange ground strokes that return the ball to the center of the court. Hitting side to side is the beginning stage of dictating play because it forces the opponent to move and creates openings for the next shot. Players can create other openings by hitting up and back.

The opening in the court might be in front of or behind the opponent. Hitting short will force the opponent to move forward and create an opening deep in the court for a lob.

Hitting to the Opponent's Weakness

If your players can hit side to side and up and back, they have the ability to exploit their opponents by hitting to their weaknesses. This could be as simple as identifying that the backhand is weaker than the forehand and directing most shots to the weaker backhand side. It may be a little more complex such as identifying a weakness in one of the opponent's shots. For example, if the opponent has a weak overhead smash, your player could hit a short ball to draw the opponent to the net and then hit a lob so the opponent is forced to either hit an overhead or retreat to the backcourt to play the shot after the ball lands.

Hitting to the opponent's weakness is a tactic that can be used effectively by the aggressive baseline player, the all-court player, or the attacking player. These players play to the weakness to force a weak return from the opponent and set up an easy shot. The aggressive baseline player will try to end the point from a weak return with a strong ground stroke. The all-court player can hit an approach shot, a sharp-angle ground stroke, or a drop shot. The attacking player will hit an approach shot and get to the net to win the point with a volley or overhead.

Playing to One's Strengths

Your players should take every opportunity to play to their strengths. For example, if one of your players can win points with a powerful forehand ground stroke, he should try to play shots that will force the opponent to hit weak shots so he can run to and set up for a point-ending forehand ground stroke.

Keep in mind, however, that your players' strengths are not limited to just strokes; their strengths can also be their styles of play, as you learned previously. As a coach, you should help your players determine their strengths and develop them based on their individual styles of play. Every style of play is effective if executed well.

Doubles Play

In tennis, doubles play is when two players cover the same side of the court and play against two opposing players, who cover the court on the opposite side of the net. The best doubles teams understand the strengths and weaknesses of both their position and the opponent's position and can work as a team to create court openings.

Starting Positions for Doubles Play

In doubles play, four starting positions are constant: the server, the server's partner, the receiver, and the receiver's partner. Each player on the court has a specific position, as shown in figure 8.1 and as described in the following sections.

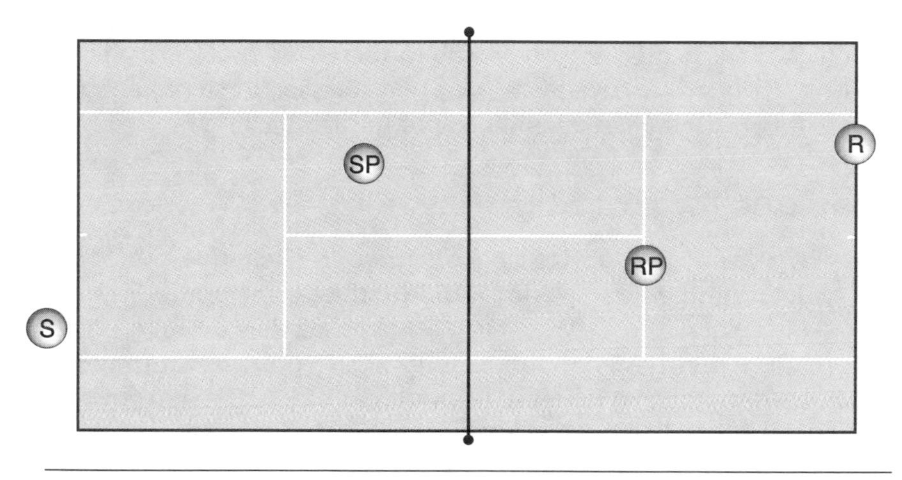

Figure 8.1 Players' starting positions for doubles.

Server

The server (S) is positioned halfway between the center mark and the doubles sideline to serve. After she hits the serve, she positions herself at the baseline for the return, moves quickly forward to volley the return, or is ready to move forward to hit an approach shot if the return is short. The server is responsible for keeping track of the score and calling out the score before serving. Servers in doubles should attempt to get at least 80 percent of their first serves in play.

Server's Partner

The server's partner (SP) is positioned at the net halfway between the center service line and the doubles sideline and midway between the net and the service line. This player is in a volley-ready position and should be thinking about hitting accurate volleys and overhead smashes to win points for his team. He should have targets in mind before the opponent hits the return.

Receiver

The receiver (R) is positioned at about the baseline along a line from the server through the middle of the service court. If the serve is hit hard, that position will be a step or two farther back in the court. If the serve lacks pace, the receiver can move a step or two inside the baseline. This player's responsibility is to hit the serve back in play, preferably away from the player at the net and back to the server. The receiver then prepares for the next return at the baseline or moves forward to the net if the serve forced her to move forward to make the return.

Receiver's Partner

The receiver's partner (RP) is positioned at the service line and about 4 feet from the center service line. This player faces the server's partner, who is at the net. The receiver's partner must be ready to react very quickly if the server's partner hits a volley or an overhead. He can also assist the receiver by calling the serve out because he has a good view of the service line.

Formations for Doubles Play

Doubles players must learn the basics of offensive and defensive court positioning before determining the specific formation they will assume. Your players must be aware that when they are close to the net, they are in an offensive position because they have the opportunity to end points by hitting the ball hard and down into the court, away from the opponents. When your players are in the backcourt, behind the baseline, they are in a defensive position, especially if one or both of the opponents are at the net. Players in a defensive position must play shots to neutralize the opponents' strength by hitting lobs over the opposing players at the net.

The following sections describe the five most common formations for doubles play used at the youth level.

One Up and One Back

In the one up and one back formation, one player is at the net and the other is in the backcourt (see figure 8.2). This formation is generally considered the most basic formation for youth doubles because, depending on how shots play out, players can quickly transition into other positions, such as two players up or two players back. In addition, most play begins from this formation (the server and receiver are at the baseline, the server's partner is at the net, and the receiver's partner is on the service line). Once play begins, the only change is that the receiver's partner will move forward to the net position after the serve is returned to the backcourt.

This formation has one player on each team in a defensive position and one player on each team in an offensive position at the net. Play will generally continue with the backcourt players exchanging ground strokes until one of the net players can intercept a ground stroke and hit a volley that lands between the two players on the opposing team. An aggressive player in the backcourt will take advantage of the first short ball and hit an approach shot and move forward to join his partner at the net. One of the weaknesses of this formation, however, is the large opening between partners. For this reason the player at the net must be aggressive to increase his opportunities to volley

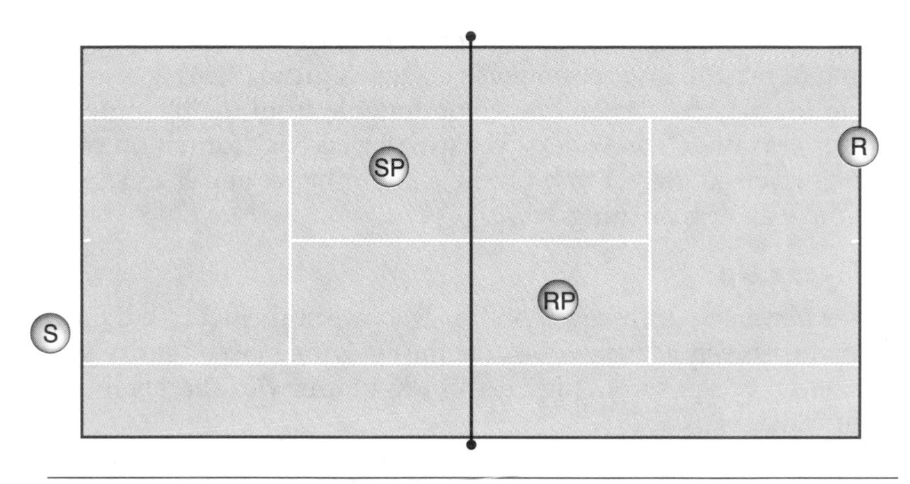

Figure 8.2 One up and one back formation.

from the net position. A well-placed volley between the opponents or to the side of the opposing net player will generally win the point.

If your players are being attacked by two players at the net, they can drop back so that both players are at the baseline. This will give them more time for their returns and take away the large opening between them when they are one up and one back. Two players in the backcourt can vary lobs and ground strokes until they force an error or until they get a short ball to hit between, outside, or over the opponents.

Two Players Back

In the two players back formation, both of your players are positioned in the backcourt (see figure 8.3). This formation puts your players in the ultimate defensive position and allows them to be ready to cover the entire court. Players in this formation return as many balls as possible and attempt to create errors by the opponents by forcing them to hit harder and closer to the lines.

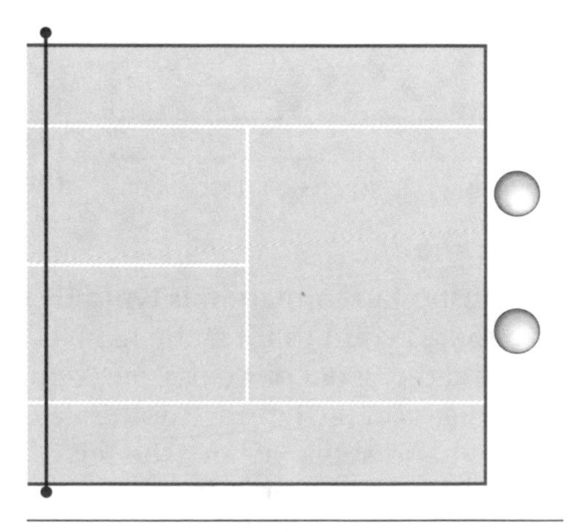

Figure 8.3 Two players back formation.

This formation is typically used by the returning team against a team that is successful at the net. If the server is able to hit powerful and well-placed serves that result in weak returns, the player at the net can generally hit many winning volleys and overheads to end points quickly. If the returning team has both players at the baseline, the close target is gone and the opening between the two players is much smaller. Both players in the backcourt have more time to react to and return volleys and overheads. This is also a good formation for players who are more comfortable from the baseline hitting ground strokes rather than volleys. The two players back formation generally forces the players at the net to hit more shots at better angles to win points because there are less openings.

Two Players Up

In the two players up formation, both players are at the net (see figure 8.4). This formation is very aggressive because the net is the most offensive position possible. From this position, players can win points with sharply hit volleys and overheads.

This formation is generally used by the serving team. The server moves forward after the serve so both players are in the net position. Two players at the net against a team in the one up and one back position can hit to the side of the closest player and win points quickly. The receiving team can also get to the two up position when the receiver moves forward after playing the service return. This generally happens when the serve lands short in the court so the receiver is moving forward during the hit and continues forward to the net after the return.

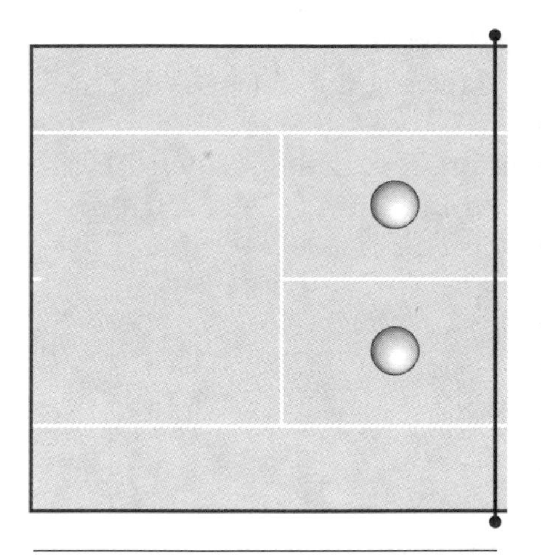

Figure 8.4 Two players up formation.

As the skill level of your players increases, you will want to take every opportunity to position doubles players at the net in an offensive position to cover their court. This puts pressure on the opponents, who now must hit to small openings between the net players, hit outside the players and inside the sidelines, or lob over their heads.

Australian

The Australian formation is typically used by the serving team when serving into the ad court to force the receiver to hit a return down the line. This will get the receiver out of a crosscourt return pattern so he must think more about placement on the return. Another reason to play this formation is that it sets up forehand shots by both the server's partner at the net and the server after putting the ball in play. In this formation, the server and the server's partner start on the same half of the court (see figure 8.5). The server begins more toward the center mark, and the partner is at the net directly in front of the server. Once the serve is hit, the net player covers the left side of the court and the server moves to cover the right side of the court.

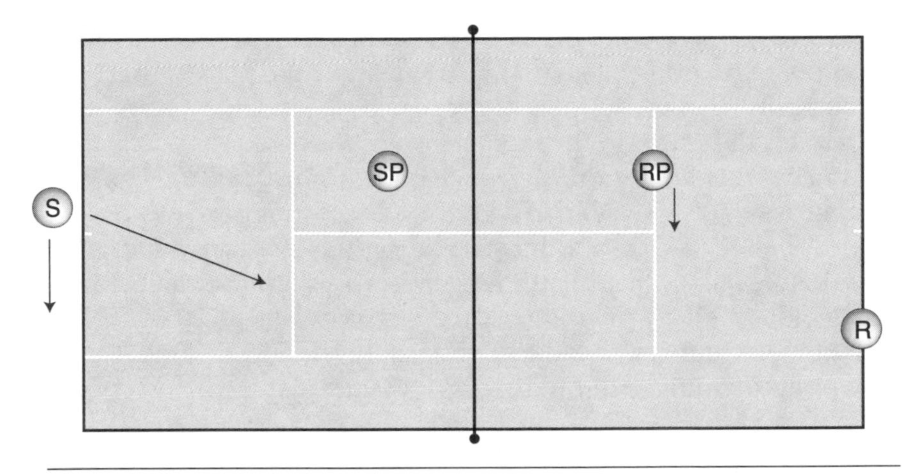

Figure 8.5 Australian formation.

This formation forces the returning team to adjust the return from a high-percentage crosscourt return to a lower-percentage down-the-line return. The down-the-line shot forces the receiver to change the angle of the serve and hit over the highest part of the net and into the shortest length of the court. Simply setting up in the Australian formation could be enough to get the receiver to overthink and disrupt her established pattern or rhythm.

I Formation

The I formation is used by the serving team to get the receiving team to watch the serving team until the last instant before making the return. In the I formation, the server begins the point by standing close to the center mark; the server's partner is at the net in a volley position directly in the center of the court and generally a few steps inside the service line (see figure 8.6).

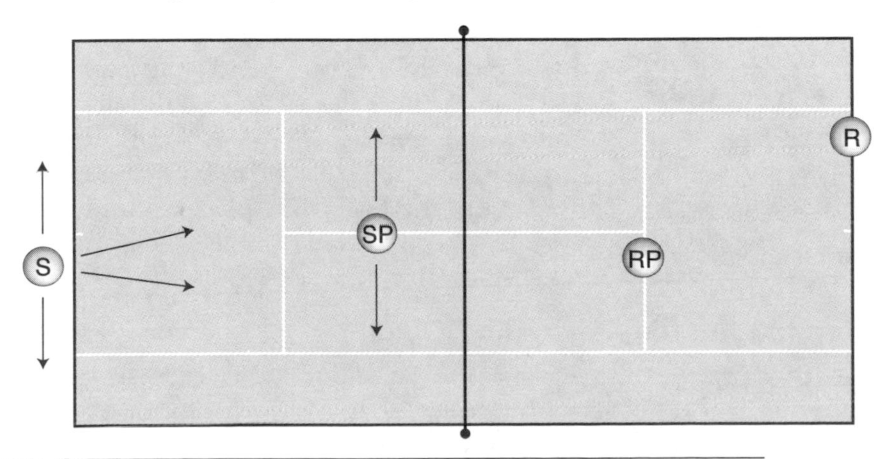

Figure 8.6 I formation.

Once the serve is hit, the net player then moves to one side or the other and the server moves to the opposite side. This disrupts the players on the receiving team because they must watch to see which side the net player is covering so they can hit the return to the opposite side.

When using this formation, the serving team must communicate clearly so that both players are in synch and both sides of the court are covered very quickly just before the return is hit. The longer the serving team can hold its positions before the return is hit, the longer the receiver must wait before deciding which side to hit the return to. If the receiver waits too long, this might produce a service return error. If the receiver simply decides to guess, the serving team may end up with a ball hit directly at the net player for an easy volley.

Tactics for Doubles Play

Coaching tactics for doubles differs from coaching tactics for singles because doubles players have more variables available in terms of both positioning and shot selection. Regardless of the formation your players are using, the following tactics will always apply.

Keeping the Ball in Play

The most basic tactic to teach your doubles players is to simply keep the ball in play; this is similar to what they have already learned for singles. Many young doubles teams achieve success by simply striving to hit every shot back over the net until the opposing team makes an error. Because most points with novice players are lost because of errors rather than won by hitting winners, this is a good tactic for young players or those with lower skill levels.

Keeping the ball in play is also a valuable tactic for players using the two back formation. In this formation, your players have little chance of hitting shots that would win points outright and must rely on consistency and court coverage. Their goal is to get every ball back in play and wear down the opponents until they make errors. Additionally, in the one up and one back formation, the backcourt player would do well to simply keep the ball in play rather than try to hit winners from the backcourt.

Coaching Tip

In addition to keeping the ball in play, strong doubles teams are constantly on the move so that they can be in the best possible position to win points and to take away openings before their opponents can hit shots.

Avoiding the Net Player

As you learned previously, a player at the net is in the most offensive position and can typically win points with a volley or an overhead smash. Because of this, your players should strive to keep the ball away from opponents at the net. For example, a player in the backcourt should try to hit crosscourt over the net or lob the ball over the net player.

The formations that are most likely to want to avoid net players are the two back formation and the one up and one back formation. In addition to trying to keep the ball in play, players in these formations are also working to hit shots away from danger by directing the ball away from the player at the net. A player deep in the backcourt should try to direct the ball away from the net player and back to the opponent in the backcourt (deep to deep).

The second way to avoid the net player is for a player(s) at the baseline to lob over the player at the net. A well-placed lob can keep the net player from hitting a shot that could end the point. This tactic is actually the best option when playing against the two up formation, but it can be used when only one player is at the net, as well.

Hitting to the Opponent's Weakness

If your doubles players can identify an opponent's weakness, they should take every opportunity to exploit it. For example, if your players learn that an opponent at the net is uncomfortable hitting volleys, your backcourt player can hit directly at the net player and force him to volley.

Hitting to a weakness can be taken to an even higher level when more specific weaknesses can be detected. This is done either by scouting opponents when they are playing matches or having your players look for and identify weaknesses during the warm-up. For example, a player might be comfortable at the net on most shots but really struggle with a high backhand volley. If so, your players should hit to that weakness every time they have the opportunity.

Hitting to the Weakest Player

Another tactic is to identify the weaker player on the opposing team and hit as many shots as possible to that player. In addition, teams can hit to the player who is in the weaker position. For example, if a player gets caught in the middle of the court and is neither at the baseline nor at the net, a good team will exploit the bad court position and force that player to play most of the shots, which typically land at the feet of a player in this position.

Playing to One's Strengths

Good doubles teams recognize their own strengths and position themselves to take advantage of them. They also strive to dictate play so they can play as many shots from their strongest positions. For example, if both players have excellent volleys and overheads, they should take every opportunity to move to the net to hit these shots. Some players are much more comfortable at the baseline and can hit accurate ground strokes and lobs, even under pressure. Those players are most effective if they stay back at the baseline and play the shots they are most comfortable hitting.

As a coach, your job is to help young doubles players determine their best skills and formations. Once they understand their team strengths, they can play their best shots from a formation that best suits their skills.

9

Coaching on Match Day

Matches provide the opportunity for your players to show what they've learned in practice. Just as your players' focus shifts on match days from learning and practicing to competing, your focus shifts from teaching skills to coaching players as they perform those skills in matches. Of course, the match is a teaching opportunity as well, but the focus is on performing what has been learned, participating, and having fun.

In previous chapters you learned how to teach your players basic tennis skills; in this chapter you will learn how to coach your players as they execute those skills in matches. We provide important coaching principles that will guide you before, during, and after the match.

Creating a Game Plan

Just as you need a practice plan for what you will cover at each practice, you also need a game plan for match day. Your game plan will vary depending on the age group you are working with. As you begin planning and mapping out how your match days will progress, keep the following age-related points in mind.

Age group	Tips
8 and under	• Encourage players to do their best. • Focus on helping players develop their individual skills for competition. The strengths and weaknesses of the opposition are of little concern at this age. • Although the use of games is important, don't have your players spend too much time just playing games. Take time for proper skill instruction.
10 and under	• Focus on helping your players execute the skills they have learned. • Encourage players to use simple defensive strategies that make it easy to play with each other and execute the techniques and skills learned in practice. • Remind players of one offensive and one defensive aspect they have learned and have them focus on these during the match.
12 and under and above	• Players should begin to focus on one or two of their opponents' strengths and weaknesses and be able to take advantage of them. • Players will sometimes adjust their play based on their opponents, but it is still most important that they properly execute the techniques and skills learned in practice. • Players use more complex offenses and defenses that will take advantage of their opponents' weaknesses.

Before the Match

Many coaches focus only on how they will coach during the actual match, when instead they should begin preparing well before the first serve of the match. Ideally, a day or two before a match, you should cover several things—in addition to techniques and tactics—to prepare your players for the match. Depending on the age group you are working with, you will need to create specific game plans for the opponents based on any information you have; make decisions on specific tactics to use; and discuss prematch details such as what to eat before the match, what to wear, and when to be at the courts.

Determining Match Tactics

Some coaches burn the midnight oil as they devise complex plans of attack. Tactics at this level, however, don't need to be complex—especially at the younger levels. The focus for the players should be on getting to position, keeping the ball in play, getting 50 percent of first serves in, and making quality returns. As you become more familiar with your players' tendencies and abilities, you can help them focus on specific tactics that will help them play better. For example, if your players have a tendency to stand around and watch the action, emphasize moving more and preparing for returns. If they are active and moving throughout play, but they are often out of position, focus partners on moving in conjunction with one another (see chapter 8).

Making Lineup Decisions

Depending on the format used in your league, you will probably need to make some decisions as to who will play in what position. You'll need to decide who will play singles, who will play doubles and with whom, and in what order your players will compete. Intrasquad scrimmages will help you determine your players' relative order of ability, which in turn will help you set your lineup. Remember, one component of the USTA Jr. Team Tennis philosophy is equal play, so make sure everyone plays in each team competition, either singles or doubles.

Because it is important that your players understand what you expect of them during matches, be clear about this in the days leading up to a match. Take time at the beginning or end of each practice to discuss these expectations. During the week before a match, inform players of the tactics that you think will work and that you plan to use in the match. Based on the age level, experience, and knowledge of your players, you may want to let them help you determine the tactics to use in the match. Your role is to help youngsters grow through the sport experience. Accepting input from your players helps them learn the game, involves them at a planning level often reserved solely for the coach, and gives them a feeling of ownership. Rather than just "carrying out orders" from the coach, they're executing the plan of attack that they helped decide. Youngsters who have a say in how they approach a task often respond with more enthusiasm and motivation.

Handling Prematch Details

Your team and their opponents will get the most out of the match experience if the competition is well organized and well run. On match day, players need to know what to do before a match: what they should eat and when, what clothing they should wear to the match, what equipment they should bring, and what time they should arrive at the courts. Discuss these particulars with them at the practice before a match. The following sections offer guidelines for discussing these issues.

Coaching Tip

For upcoming competitions, at least a week ahead of time, confirm court availability with the staff of the facility where you will be playing. Contact the opposing coach at least two days before your teams are to play to confirm the date and time of the competition, directions to the tennis facility, the number of courts to be used, and the schedule of play.

Prematch Meal

In general, the goal of the prematch meal is to fuel the athlete for the upcoming event, to maximize carbohydrate stores (which are easily digested and absorbed and are a ready source of fuel), and to provide energy to the brain. We suggest that athletes consume foods that are easily digested, such as carbohydrate and protein, rather than those that are digested slowly, such as fat. Good carbohydrate foods include spaghetti, cereal, and rice. Good protein foods include low-fat yogurt and boneless, skinless chicken. Athletes should eat foods that they are familiar with and that they know they can digest easily. Big meals should be eaten three to four hours before the contest to allow the stomach to empty completely. Athletes who don't have time for a regular meal can occasionally use sports beverages and meal-replacement bars instead, but these shouldn't be used regularly as a replacement for the prematch meal.

That said, the match time will determine what type of meal your athletes should consume. If your match time is right after school or early on a weekend morning, it won't be possible or practical for your players to eat three to four hours before the match. A lighter snack or breakfast will be more appropriate in these situations.

Clothing and Equipment

Unless the team is traveling a long distance to play, you should typically require that your players arrive in their team uniforms (as described in more detail in chapter 3, the team uniform typically consists of matching T-shirts and shorts) and nonmarking shoes designed for tennis. Each player should bring a racket, tennis balls, and a water bottle (be sure to discuss equipment expectations at the preseason parent orientation meeting, as described in chapter 2). Make sure you have extra rackets in case a player breaks a string.

Players may also find that other items such as sunscreen, hats, wristbands, and towels may also be useful during competitions. Make sure that eyeglasses or sunglasses fit snugly on any players wearing them. If they don't, ask parents to provide their children with an elastic sport strap to hold them in place. Players should be allowed to wear braces or protective wraps to prevent injury or protect current injuries, as long as they are cleared by a doctor to participate. Ask parents to ensure that their children are wearing any of these items properly when they come to the match—you can't be responsible for the maintenance or fit of such devices.

Coaching Tip
Teams with players in the older age groups may routinely play doubleheaders or multiple-match tournaments. In such situations players must stay hydrated and fueled during play, not just before. Consider working with parents to rotate the responsibility for providing water or sports drinks, along with nutritious snacks such as fruit or crackers, for longer competitions. See also chapter 4 for guidelines on how much fluid your players should drink before, during, and after a contest.

Arrival Time

Your players need to warm up adequately before a match, so instruct them to arrive 20 to 40 minutes before match time, depending on the age level, to go through the team warm-up (see the following section, Warm-Up). Following are the suggested arrival times for each age group:

- 8 and under—20 minutes
- 10 and under—30 minutes
- 12 and under and above—40 minutes

Designate where you want the team to gather as they arrive so you can quickly see who is there and can start the warm-up efficiently. If you have problems with players coming late to matches, consider making a team rule stating that players must show up a designated amount of time before the match and go through the complete team warm-up.

Warm-Up

Players need to both physically and mentally prepare for a match once they arrive. Physical preparation involves warming up. We've suggested that players arrive 20 to 40 minutes before the match to warm up, depending on the age level, with younger players arriving closer to match time to keep them

Coaching Tip
Although the site coordinator has formal responsibilities for facilities and equipment, you should know what to look for to ensure that the match is safe for all athletes (see the Facilities and Equipment Checklist in appendix A on page 154). Arrive at the match site 45 to 60 minutes before the match so you can check the facility, check in with the site coordinator and greet your players as they arrive to warm up.

focused and not too tired from the excitement of warming up and getting ready to play.

The warm-up should consist of a few brief games or drills that focus on skills such as serving, receiving, and rallying (for example, rallying foam balls to get the players running and hitting). The warm-up should also include stretches and range of motion exercises.

Help your players prepare mentally for the match by reminding them of the skills they've been working on in recent practices and focusing their attention on their strengths and what they've been doing well. Refrain from delivering a long-winded pep talk. Instead, take time to remind players that they should work as a team, play hard and smart, and have fun!

Unplanned Events

Part of being prepared to coach is expecting the unexpected. What do you do when players are late? What if you have an emergency and can't make the match or will be late? What if the match is rained out or otherwise postponed? Being prepared to handle out-of-the-ordinary circumstances will help you if and when unplanned events happen.

If players are late, you may have to adjust your team lineup. Although this may not be a major inconvenience, stress to your players that there are important reasons for being on time. First, part of being a member of a team is being committed to and responsible for the other members. When players don't show up, or show up late, they break that commitment. And second, players need to go through a warm-up to prepare physically for the match. Skipping the warm-up risks injury.

If an emergency causes you to be late or miss a match, notify your assistant coach, if you have one, or the league coordinator. If notified in advance, a parent of a player or another volunteer might be able to step in for the match.

Sometimes a match will be postponed because of inclement weather or for other reasons such as unsafe court conditions. If the postponement takes place before match day, call every member of your team to let them know. If it happens while the teams are on-site and preparing for the match, gather your team members and explain why the match has been postponed. Make sure all of your players have a ride home before you leave. You should be the last to leave.

Communicating With Parents

You have already laid the groundwork for your communication with parents at the preseason parent orientation meeting, where you explained the best ways they can support their kids'—and the whole team's—efforts on the court. Hopefully you explained the importance of judging success based not just on the outcome of the match but also on how the kids are improving their performances.

If parents yell at the kids for mistakes they make during the match, make disparaging remarks about the opponents, or shout instructions, ask them to refrain and to instead support the players through their comments and actions. You have most likely explained these standards of conduct at the preseason parent orientation, but some parents may need reminders.

When time permits, as parents gather before a match and before the players have approached the court, you can let them know in a general sense what the players have been focusing on during the past week and what your goals are for the match. However, your players must come first during this time, so focus on your players during the prematch warm-up.

After a match, quickly come together as a staff and decide what to say to the players and then informally assess with parents, as the opportunity arises, how the players did based not on the outcome but on meeting performance goals and playing to the best of their abilities. Help parents see the contest as a process, not solely as a test that is pass/fail or win/lose. Encourage parents to reinforce that concept at home.

For more information on communicating with parents, see page 15 of chapter 2.

During the Match

Throughout the match, you must keep the competition in proper perspective and help your players do the same. You will observe how your players execute skills and how well they play together. These observations will help you decide appropriate practice plans for the following week. Let's take a more detailed look at your responsibilities during a match.

Tactical Decisions

Although you may not be called on to create a complex match strategy, as mentioned before, you may have to make tactical decisions in several areas throughout a match. You may have to make slight adjustments to your players' tactics or deal with players' performance errors. Let's take a look at these in more detail.

Keeping a Proper Perspective

Winning matches is the short-term goal of your tennis program. Helping your players learn the techniques, tactics, and rules of tennis; how to become fit; and how to be good sports in tennis and in life are the long-term goals. Your young athletes are "winning" when they are becoming better human beings through their participation in tennis. Keep that perspective in mind when you coach. You have the privilege of setting the tone for how your team approaches the match. Keep winning and all aspects of the competition in proper perspective, and your young charges will likely follow suit.

Adjusting Players' Tactics

For the 8 and under and 10 and under age groups, you probably won't adjust tactics too significantly during a match. Rather, you'll focus on the basic tactics, and you'll emphasize the specific tactics your players need to work on. However, coaches of players 12 and under and above may have to make tactical adjustments to improve their players' chances of performing well and winning. Before a match begins, assess the opponents' styles of play and tactics and make appropriate adjustments—that is, those that your players are prepared for and have learned in practice. You may want to consider the following examples when adjusting tactics:

- How does the opponent usually play? Is the opponent a serve and volleyer, counter-puncher, or all-court player? This can help you make play adjustments.
- What are the opponent's strengths and weaknesses? As you identify them, suggest that your player hit to the opponent's weaknesses and avoid the opponent's strengths.
- Is the opponent an all-court player? Is she quick and athletic, with no major strengths or weaknesses? Is she in excellent physical condition, or does she get tired after a few long points? The opponent's style of play should influence how you prepare a player for a match.

Knowing the answers to such questions can help you formulate a match plan and make adjustments during play. It will also help your players adapt their play to their strengths. However, don't stress tactics too much during a match. Doing so can take the fun out of the sport for the players. If you don't trust your memory, carry a pen and pad to note which individual skills or tactics need attention at the next practice. Additionally, although USTA Jr. Team Tennis allows coaching during matches, some tennis leagues do not. Check your league rules for its position on match coaching.

Correcting Players' Errors

In chapter 6 you learned about two types of errors: learning errors and performance errors. Learning errors are those that occur because athletes don't know how to perform a skill. Performance errors are made not because athletes don't know how to execute the skill but because they make mistakes in carrying out what they do know.

Determining which type of error your athletes are making is not always easy. Knowing their capabilities can help you determine whether they know the skills and are simply making mistakes in executing them or if they don't know how to perform them. If they are making learning errors—that is, they don't know how to perform the skills—note this and cover them at the next practice. Match time is not the time to teach skills.

If your players are making performance errors, however, you can help them correct them during play. Players who make performance errors often do so because they have a lapse in concentration or motivation, or they are simply demonstrating human error. Fear of competition can also adversely affect a young player's technique, and a word of encouragement about concentration may help. If you do decide to correct a performance error during a match, do so in a quiet, controlled, and positive tone of voice during a break or when the player is on the sidelines with you.

When a player makes a performance error, you must determine whether it is just an occasional error that anyone could make or whether it is an expected error for a youngster at that stage of development. If the latter is the case, then the player may appreciate your not commenting on the mistake. The player knows it was a mistake and may already know how to correct it. On the other hand, perhaps an encouraging word and a "coaching cue" (such as "remember to follow through on your shots") may be just what the player needs. Knowing the players and what to say is very much a part of the art of coaching.

Coaching Tip

Designate an area where players should go after coming off the court. In this area, you can speak to them either individually or as a group and make necessary adjustments.

Coach and Player Behavior

Another aspect of coaching on match day is managing behavior—both yours and your athletes'. It is your responsibility, as a coach, to control emotions when aspects of the match, such as your tactics, are not working as you or your players had hoped.

Coach Conduct

You very much influence your players' behavior before, during, and after a match. If you're up, your players are more likely to be up. If you're anxious, they'll take notice, and the anxiety can become contagious. If you're negative, they'll respond with worry. If you're positive, they'll play with more enjoyment. If you're constantly yelling instructions or commenting on mistakes and errors, they will have difficulty concentrating. Instead, let players get into the flow of the match.

The focus should be on positive competition and having fun. A coach who overorganizes everything and dominates play from the sidelines is definitely not making the contest fun. So how should you conduct yourself? Here are a few pointers:

- Be calm, in control, and supportive of your players.
- Encourage players often, and instruct during play sparingly. Players should focus on their performances during matches, not on instructions shouted from the sidelines.
- If you need to instruct a player, do so during a break or when you're both on the sidelines together, in an unobtrusive manner. Never yell at players for making mistakes. Instead, briefly demonstrate or remind them of the correct technique and encourage them. Tell them how to correct the problem on the court.

Before your first match, discuss sideline demeanor as a staff and ensure that everyone is in agreement about how they will conduct themselves on the sidelines. Then stick with your agreement. Remember, you're not playing in the US Open! Youth tennis competitions are designed to help players develop their skills and themselves—and have fun. So coach at matches in a manner that helps your players achieve these things.

Player Conduct

You're responsible for keeping your players under control. Do so by setting a good example and by disciplining when necessary. Set team rules for good behavior. If players attempt to cheat, fight, argue, badger, yell disparaging remarks, and the like, it is your responsibility to correct the misbehavior. It is important to remember, too, that younger players are still learning how to deal with their emotions in addition to learning the game. As a coach, you must strive to remain calm when young players are having trouble controlling their emotions.

Consider team rules in these areas of match conduct:

- Player language
- Player behavior
- Discipline for misbehavior
- Dress code for competitions
- Calling lines
- Announcing the score

Player Welfare

Some athletes attach their self-worth to winning and losing. This idea is fueled by coaches, parents, peers, and society, who place great emphasis on winning. Players become anxious when they're not sure they can meet the expectations of others or of themselves—especially when meeting a particular expectation is important to them also.

If your players look uptight and anxious during a match, find ways to reduce both the uncertainties about how their performance will be evaluated and the importance they are attaching to the match. Help athletes focus on realistic personal goals—goals that are reachable and measurable and that will help them improve their performance while having fun as they play. Another way to reduce anxiety on match day is to stay away from emotional prematch pep talks. Instead, remind players of the skills and tactics they will use and remind them to play hard, do their best, and have fun.

When coaching during matches, remember that the most important outcome from playing tennis is self-worth. Keep that firmly in mind and strive to promote this through every coaching decision.

Opponents

Respect opponents because, without them, there wouldn't be a competition. Opponents provide opportunities for your team to test itself, improve, and excel.

You and your players should show respect for opponents by giving your best efforts and being civil. Don't allow your players to "trash talk" or taunt opponents. Such behavior is disrespectful to others and to the spirit of the competition. Immediately remove from a match any player who disobeys your team rules in this area.

After the Match

When the match is over, join your team in congratulating the coaches and players of the opposing team. Check on any injuries players sustained and teach them how to care for them. Then, hold a brief meeting—which is explained later—to ensure that your players are on an even keel, whether they won or lost.

Reactions Following a Game

Your first concern after a match should be your players' attitudes and mental well-being. You don't want them to be too high after a win or too low after a loss. This is the time you can be most influential in helping them keep the outcome in perspective and settle their emotions.

Coaching Tip
Before conducting the postmatch team meeting, lead a cool-down similar to the one you use to end your practice sessions. This will not only help your players improve their flexibility but also help them calm down after the match and focus on what you are about to say. The younger the player, the shorter your postmatch cool-down and team meeting should be. For players 10 and under, keep the postmatch routine to no more than 10 minutes, and no more than 15 minutes for older players.

When celebrating a victory, make sure your players do so in a way that respects the opponents. It's okay and appropriate to be happy and celebrate a win, but don't allow your players to taunt the opponents or boast about their victory. If you were defeated, your players will naturally be disappointed. But, if your players have made a winning effort, let them know this. After a loss, help them keep their chins up and maintain a positive attitude that will carry over into the next practice and contest. Winning and losing are a part of life, not just a part of sport. If players can handle both equally well, they'll be successful in whatever they do.

Postmatch Team Meeting

Following the match, gather your team in a designated area for a short meeting. Before this meeting, decide as a staff what to say and who will say it. Be sure that the staff speaks with one voice following the match.

If your players have performed well in a match, compliment them and congratulate them. Tell them specifically what they did well, whether they won or lost. This will reinforce their desire to repeat their good performances. Don't use this time to criticize individual players for poor performances in front of teammates or attempt to go over tactical problems and adjustments. The time to help players improve their skills is at the next practice, not immediately after a match, because they won't absorb much tactical information at this time.

Finally, make sure your players have transportation home. Be the last one to leave to ensure that your players are fully supervised.

10

Developing Season and Practice Plans

We hope you've learned a lot from this book—what your responsibilities are as a coach, how to communicate well and provide for safety, how to teach and shape skills, and how to coach on match days. But match days make up only a portion of your season. You and your players will spend more time in practices than in competition. How well you conduct practices and prepare your players for competition will greatly affect not only your players' enjoyment and success throughout the season but also your own.

Fun Learning Environment

Regardless of what point you're at in your season, work to create an environment that welcomes learning and promotes teamwork. Following are seven tips to help you and your staff get the most out of your practices:

1. Stick to the practice times agreed on as a staff.
2. Start and end each practice as a team.
3. Keep the practice routine as consistent as possible so the players can feel comfortable.
4. Be organized in your approach by moving quickly from one activity to another and from one stage of training to another.
5. Tell your players what the practice will include before the practice starts.
6. Allow the players to take water breaks whenever possible.
7. Focus on providing positive feedback.

In addition to trying the drills provided throughout chapter 7, you may also want to consider using other activities to add variety and make practices more fun. In appendix C on page 163 you will find 21 tennis activities that, when used during practice, will help prepare your players for many situations that arise in competition.

Season Plans

Your season plan acts as a snapshot of the entire season. Before the first practice with your players, you must sit down as a staff and develop such a plan. To do so, simply write down each practice and game date; then go back and number the practices. These practice numbers are the foundation of your season plan. Now you can work through the plan, moving from practice to practice, and outline what you hope to achieve by noting the purpose of the practice, the main skills you will cover, and the activities you will use.

Following is more detailed information about season plans for four age groups for USTA Jr. Team Tennis: 8 and under, 10 and under, 12 and under, and 14 and under. Remember, however, that part of the art of coaching is being able to adjust your plan if the situation warrants it. You may need to adjust your plans to accommodate the skill level of your players; don't rely solely on the players' ages to develop your plan. For example, you might use the 10 and under plan for a team of 11- and 12-year-olds who are new to tennis; conversely, if you live in an area where leagues start at age 8, you might use the 12 and under plan for a group of experienced 10-year-olds who have already been playing tennis for several years. Similarly, if your players are having trouble with specific skills, you might adjust your season plan to allow more practice time for those skills. Or, if your players are bored because they've already learned the skills you're introducing, don't be afraid to adjust your plan to allow time for teaching new tactics.

Coaching Tip

While developing your season plan, keep in mind that you will want to incorporate the games approach into your practices. As you learned in chapter 5, the games approach is superior to the traditional approach because it focuses on replicating the game environment. Using matchlike activities better prepares the players, both physically and mentally, for the demands of the game.

Season Plan for Players 8 and Under

Players in this age group need to learn the basics of how to play the game. You will need to teach the rules, scoring, and lines and focus on simple receiving and sending skills. Once your players have mastered these skills, introduce them to the underhand serve and service return. Tactics for this age group include keeping the ball in play, moving the opponent from side to side, and hitting to the opponent's weak side.

Practice	Purpose
1	Introduce the game of tennis. Teach players to control the racket and ball. Introduce the forehand ground stroke with control, direction, and depth.
2	Introduce the backhand ground stroke with control, direction, and depth. Review the forehand ground stroke and the low-to-high swing.
3	Review the forehand and backhand ground strokes. Introduce the underhand serve.
4	Introduce the service return and basic court positioning after shots from the baseline.
5	Review rally consistency using random forehands and backhands. Review the consistency, direction, depth, and height of ground strokes.
6	Introduce the volley and contact point on both the forehand and backhand sides. Emphasize preparation, quick movement, and placement.
7	Introduce playing and scoring, including match play and good sporting behavior.
8	Teach singles positioning and tactics, including moving the opponent, hitting to an opponent's weakness, and playing to their own strengths.

Season Plan for Players 10 and Under

Players in this age group are still developing the skills necessary to play a complete game, including skills on both the forehand and backhand sides, serves and returns, volleys, overheads from the net, and lobs from the backcourt. You will also introduce the overhand service motion to players in this group.

Practice	Purpose
1	Introduce the forehand ground stroke. Emphasize contact point, consistency, direction, depth, height, spin, and speed.
2	Introduce the backhand ground stroke. Emphasize contact point, consistency, direction, depth, height, spin, and speed.
3	Introduce the overhand serve using targets for direction, speed, and spin.
4	Introduce the service return, focusing on consistency, direction, and positioning.
5	Introduce net play, including forehand and backhand volleys and the overhead smash.
6	Introduce approaching the net, including recognition of a short ball and hitting approach shots and approach volleys.
7	Teach singles tactics and positioning, including keeping the ball in play, moving the opponent from side to side and up and back, and hitting to a weakness.
8	Teach doubles positioning and tactics, including the responsibilities of each player.

Season Plan for Players 12 and Under

Players in this age group continue to refine all the skills necessary to play complete matches from every area of the court. These players should begin to determine which style of play best suits their skills and temperaments and develop the strengths necessary to build on their style.

Practice	Purpose
1	Teach rally skills using the forehand ground stroke. Introduce tracking, movement, and contact point. Emphasize direction, height, and depth.
2	Teach rally skills using the backhand and forehand ground strokes. Introduce the backhand and the backhand contact point. Emphasize direction, height, and depth.
3	Introduce the serve and return. Introduce the basics of the overhand serving motion and the three target areas for the serve. Emphasize service return positioning and shortening the backswing because of the quicker reaction time.
4	Introduce volleys and net play, including volleys on both the forehand and backhand sides as well as direction and depth.
5	Introduce the overhead smash at the net and the lob from the baseline.
6	Introduce approaching the net. Players should learn when to move forward for a short ball, how to execute a proper approach shot, and how to move into the best position at the net to finish points with a volley or overhead.
7	Introduce basic singles tactics and proper court positioning after hitting a shot.
8	Introduce players to basic doubles positioning and the responsibilities of each player on a doubles team, both serving and receiving.

Season Plan for Players 14 and Under

These players have developed the basic skills of the game and need to keep refining their strokes, especially the use of spins and speed. Players in this age group must develop a solid tactical foundation for both singles and doubles play. They should understand court positioning and shot direction and have the ability to exploit an opponent's weakness and play to their own strengths.

Practice	Purpose
1	Review forehand and backhand ground strokes and the use of the five controls.
2	Review serving and the use of targets, spin, and speed.
3	Review the service return and the differences between returning a first and second serve.
4	Review net play and the offensive skills needed to play offensive volleys and overheads, including direction, spin, and speed. Review lobs, emphasizing consistency, height, direction, and depth. Review the overhead smash, stressing consistency and direction.
5	Review approaching the net, understanding when to move forward, and playing both approach shots and approach volleys.
6	Review singles play, including positioning, shot selection, recovery, and styles of play.
7	Review doubles play, including basic doubles positioning and variations depending on the strengths and weaknesses of the opponents.
8	Review match play, including preparation, good sporting behavior, mental toughness, staying focused, and being the best doubles partner.

Practice Plans

Coaches rarely believe they have enough time to cover everything they want to cover. Practice plans will help you organize your thoughts so you stay on track toward your practice objectives and help you better visualize and prepare so you can run your practices effectively.

First, your practice plans should be appropriate for the age group and skill level of the players you are coaching and should incorporate all the skills and concepts presented in that age group's season plan. To begin, each practice plan should note the practice objective (which is drawn from your season plan) and the equipment necessary to execute the specific practice. Each practice plan should also include a warm-up and cool-down. Remember that during the cool-down you should attend to any injuries suffered during practice and make sure the players drink plenty of water.

Sample Practice Plan for Players 8 and Under

Objective

To introduce the return of serve

Equipment

Foam balls; 17-, 19-, 21-, and 23-inch rackets; pop-up net or caution tape to create a temporary net; chalk tape or throw-down lines to mark the court; eight cones

Activity	Description	Coaching points
Prepractice meeting (5 min.)	Take roll call and explain the purpose of the practice (to introduce the return of serve).	• Make eye contact with every player.
Warm-up (10 min.)	Players warm up by doing a series of movement activities, as follows: • Players run forward and touch the ground with both hands, keeping their backs straight. They do the same after moving backward and to the right and left. • In pairs, players throw a ball back and forth beginning with an underhand toss and ending with an overhand throw. • Figure-eight agility drill—Each player moves quickly through a set of two cones placed 5 and 10 feet in front, moving forward and sideways in a figure-eight pattern. • Reaction speed drill—Each player faces a partner and one player signals with the hand for the partner to change direction (right, left, forward, and backward). The player must change direction quickly after each signal and stay balanced with the eyes and head forward.	• Loosens up muscles • Improves core body strength • Improves agility and balance • Develops the balanced action of tossing by using the opposite arm and leg • Develops trunk rotation and high arm action on the overhand throw • Improves reflexes • Prepares muscles for running and hitting
Review the underhand serve (10 min.)	Demonstrate the feet position, the drop of the ball to the racket, and the path of the racket for the underhand serve. After the players are positioned on the court, rotate to help each player by correcting, demonstrating, and praising.	• Check the proper position of the feet. • Make sure the backswing is behind and to the side. • Strings should face the court and be open at the point of contact. • The forward swing should move through the ball toward the target. • The follow-through should extend toward the target.

(continued)

Activity	Description	Coaching points
Positioning for the return of serve (3 min.)	The receiver will be halfway from where the ball could go right and left and still be in the court, and halfway between the typical first and second bounce.	• Show where the first and second bounce typically land by placing balls on the court. Do the same for right and left.
Ready position (2 min.)	Demonstrate the ready position with the receiver facing the server.	• Make sure the racket is in front, knees are flexed, the weight is off the heels, and eyes are on the server.
Returning practice (10 min.)	Each player serves to a partner, who moves and hits the return back to the server.	• Emphasize the ready position. • Watch footwork. • Encourage short backswings. • Encourage good contact points. • Watch follow-through.
Serve and return game (10 min.)	Have players in pairs serving and receiving from both the deuce and ad courts. The server serves, the receiver returns, and the server catches the return to score 1 point. Change server after four serves. Each pair tries to get 11 successful serve, return, and catch sequences.	• Emphasize a good ready position. • Encourage quick movement to the ball. • Encourage short backswings. • Emphasize a controlled swing and follow-through.
Cool-down (5 min.)	Players move from line to line as you call out each line. Use different types of movements, such as walking, hopping, skipping, and walking without the heels touching the ground.	• Teaches the lines of the court • Emphasizes good balance • Lowers heart rate and body temperature
Homework (5 min.)	Players dribble soccer balls around a series of cones.	• Emphasizes balance • Encourages the use of both legs and short but quick movements

Sample Practice Plan for Players 10 and Under

Objective

To introduce the overhand serve

Equipment

Six cones; 36 low-compression balls; 21-, 23-, and 25-inch rackets; five playground or soccer balls

Activity	Description	Coaching points
Pre-practice meeting (5 min.)	Take roll call, review the previous practice, and explain the purpose of the practice (to introduce the overhand service motion).	• Make eye contact with every player. • Single out good performances. • Mention players by name who improved in the previous day's work.
Warm-up (5 min.)	Players sidestep from baseline to net and back three to five times. They should keep their backs straight and their weight forward and prevent their heels from hitting.	• Increases circulation • Loosens muscles • Improves coordination • Improves strength
Throwing in pairs (10 min.)	In pairs, have players throw a playground or soccer ball back and forth, as follows: • Players throw the ball back and forth using a two-hand chest pass. • Players throw the ball back and forth with two hands over the head. Check for knee flexion and drive. • Players throw the ball backward to a partner with two hands. Knees should bend and legs should drive to get ball high in the air. • Players throw the ball back and forth using an underhand toss. • Players throw the ball back and forth using an overhand motion.	• Encourages synchronizing legs and arms • Emphasizes catching with two hands • Teaches players to drive from the ground with the legs first, then the upper body and arms • Coordinates step and arm action with the opposite arm and leg • Encourages players to develop upper body rotation for an overhand throw • Teaches players to transfer weight from the back to the front leg
Review ground strokes (5 min.)	Demonstrate both forehand and backhand ground strokes. Emphasize a consistent contact point, good balance, and recovery after each shot. Have players rally to see which pair can hit the most consecutive ground strokes—forehand to forehand, backhand to backhand, and alternating forehand and backhand ground strokes.	• Review the stroke pattern for both the forehand and backhand. • Develops consistent rally speed • Players must work cooperatively to sustain the longest rally. • Develops quick feet and movement when hitting alternate forehand and backhand ground strokes

(continued)

Activity	Description	Coaching points
Introduce and practice the overhand service motion (15 min.)	Demonstrate the following points for the overhand serve: • Starting position for feet and racket • Arm separation • Backswing with racket and ball toss with opposite arm • Throwing action of the racket • Contact point • Follow-through Have players practice the full service motion close to the net, at the service line, and finally from the baseline. Make sure players serve into both the deuce and ad courts.	• Be sure servers are set, balanced, and relaxed before serving. • Players should start slow with the backswing and toss and accelerate through the contact point. • Players should follow through on the court in the direction of the target—not right or left. They should keep their heads and eyes up at the contact point. • Players should follow through on the opposite side of the body.
Target serves (15 min.)	Place three cones each in the deuce and ad court. Players serve two balls at a time into either the deuce or ad court. Each player scores 1 point for getting the serve into the court and 5 points for hitting a target cone. Players must call out the target before serving.	• Make sure players lift the ball with an extended arm for a consistent toss. • Players should make contact at the highest point they can reach. • Follow-through should be in the direction of the target. • Make sure players transfer their weight from the back to the front foot before contact.
Cool-down (5 min.)	After players pick up all of the balls and return them to the basket, have them do a series of static stretches.	• Lowers heart rate and body temperature • Make sure stretch repetitions are consistent.
Homework (5 min.)	Have players hit 50 good serves before the next practice.	• Reinforces service motion

Sample Practice Plan for Players 12 and Under

Objective

To introduce approaching the net

Equipment

Basket of balls; rackets; six foam balls

Activity	Description	Coaching points
Pre-practice meeting (5 min.)	Take roll call. Review the previous practice, and explain the purpose of this practice—specifically, to introduce the approach shot, or how to get from the baseline, where players hit ground strokes and lobs, to the net, where players can play more offensive volleys and overheads.	• Make eye contact with every player. • Single out good performances. • Mention players by name who improved in the previous day's work.
Warm-up (10 min.)	Players warm up, as follows: • Players hit service line to service line with foam balls, hitting alternate forehands and backhands. • One player positions at the net, and the other player positions at the service line. With foam balls, players hit every combination of forehand and backhand volleys and forehand and backhand ground strokes.	• Increases circulation • Loosens muscles • Helps players review both ground strokes and volleys • Develops direction on ground strokes and volleys • Improves reflexes
Review overheads and lobs (15 min.)	Using foam balls, a player at the service line hits two ground strokes so the player at the net can hit a forehand volley and a backhand volley. The third shot should be a lob, and the player at the net hits an overhead. Players should try to keep one ball in play at all times.Have players switch positions every two minutes.	• Emphasize short volleys with control. • Watch for good preparation and ready position. • Emphasize quick turns and positioning for the overhead. • Players should recover to a good volley position.
Introduce approach shots (25 min.)	Players practice approach shots, as follows: • Players form a single-file line behind the baseline. Toss a ball just inside the service line for each player. Each player moves forward and hits the approach shot and finishes in a ready position halfway between the service line and the net. Repeat on the backhand side. • Feed each player a short ball over the net. Each player moves forward, hits the approach shot, and moves to the net with a split step halfway between the service line and the net. Feed a second ball so the player can volley the ball into the open court. Repeat on the backhand side.	• After hitting the approach shot, players should be set at the net and ready by the time the opponent makes contact. • At contact by the opponent, the net player should get two steps in or across for the volley or three steps back for the overhead. • Players should try to end the point with the first volley or overhead after playing the approach shot.

(continued)

Activity	Description	Coaching points
Champs of the doubles court (25 min.)	Players play in teams (doubles) and all hit a series of three shots—an approach shot, a volley, and an overhead. The team winning 2 out of 3 points defends the champions position at the opposite baseline.	• Encourage positive comments. • Encourage deep approach shots and aggressive volleys and overheads. • Players should move quickly to the net after playing the overhead. • Encourage a good split step and being in a ready position by the time the opponent plays the shot.
Cool-down (10 min.)	After players pick up all of the balls and return them to the basket, have them do a series of static stretches. Do static stretches for both upper and lower body.	• Lowers heart rate and body temperature • Stretches all muscles on both sides for both the upper and lower body
Homework (15 min.)	Have players hit 10 forehands in a row, 10 backhands in a row, 10 forehand volleys in a row, and 10 backhand volleys in a row using a foam ball.	• Excellent review of basic strokes • Works on consistency and control

Sample Practice Plan for Players 14 and Under

Objective

To practice lobs and overheads

Equipment

Basket of balls; rackets; 24 foam balls; 24 low-compression balls; three boxes or wastebaskets

Activity	Description	Coaching points
Warm-up (10 min.)	Players warm up, as follows: • Players rally service line to service line hitting alternate forehand and backhand ground strokes. • Bucket head drill—Three players are at the net holding boxes or wastebaskets on their heads. Other players lob the ball from the opposite baseline, and players at the net try to catch the lobs in their buckets.	• Emphasize good footwork and consistent contact points on service-line-to-service-line rally. • Encourage players to move quickly and track the ball so the lob drops in the bucket. • Encourage quick first steps.
Ground stroke volley combination activity (15 min.)	Players work in pairs with one at the net and the other at the service line. Using foam balls, players hit 10 ground strokes and volleys. After 10 consecutive hits, the backcourt player moves between the service line and the baseline and attempts 10 in a row using low-compression balls. If successful, the player moves to the baseline for 10 consecutive ground stroke and volley combinations with regulation balls.	• Encourage controlled and accurate ground strokes. • Emphasize quick movements and setups for the volley. • Encourage accurate and controlled volleys and recoveries after each shot.
Lob and overhead activities (25 min.)	Players practice the lob and overhead, as follows: • To practice the lob, position partners halfway between the service line and baseline and have them rally high so balls land on the service line. Begin with the forehand and change to the backhand. • To practice the overhead, one player is at the net and the other lobs from the baseline. The net player moves and catches the lobs above her head with her racket hand. After several catches, the player at the net uses her racket. She reaches up and hits the ball, following through across her body to direct the overhead back to the feeder. See how long players can keep the ball going.	• Explain that if the lob is very high, it is best to play the overhead after the bounce. • Lobs should be hit so the highest point of the lob's arc is directly over the net person's head. • Explain that when moving back for the overhead, players should turn sideways for a shuffle or sidestep rather than backpedaling. • The contact point for the overhead is the same as that for the serve.

(continued)

Activity	Description	Coaching points
Team doubles (25 min.)	Players form two doubles teams. Extra players are behind the baseline on each end of the court. Points are played beginning with a serve or drop hit. After each point is played, players rotate on and off the court at each end. Players should have opportunities to play lobs and overheads frequently in doubles. Games can be played to 7 points with teams switching ends after each game. One side serves the entire game into the deuce court.	• Players behind the baseline should lob over the net person's head. • Overheads should be directed down the middle between the two players or to the side of the closest player. • After hitting the overhead, players should recover to a good ready position at the net.
Cool-down (10 min.)	After players pick up all of the balls and return them to the basket, have them do a series of static stretches.	• Lowers heart rate and body temperature • Stretches the upper and lower body on both sides
Homework (15 min.)	Have players rally against a wall, beginning each rally with a serve.	• Players should work on good preparation and service motion. • Emphasize the transition from serve to service return to rally.

Constructing practice plans requires both organization and flexibility on your part. Don't be intimidated by the number of skills and tactics you've listed in your season plan. Pick out a few basics and build your initial practice plans around them; this process will get easier after you've drafted a few plans. Then you can move from teaching simple concepts and skills to drawing up plans that introduce more complex ones. Build in some flexibility; if you find that what you've planned for practice isn't working, have a backup activity that approaches the skill or concept from a different angle. The priorities are to keep your team playing the game and to help everyone have fun while they're learning.

Appendix A

Related Checklists and Forms

This appendix contains checklists and forms that will be useful in your tennis program. All checklists and forms mentioned in the text can be found here. You may reproduce and use these checklists and forms as needed for your tennis program.

Facilities and Equipment Checklist

Court Surface

- ❑ The court is free of debris.
- ❑ The court is not wet.
- ❑ The height of the net and the height of the center strap are correct.

Outside Playing Area

- ❑ Storage sheds and facilities are locked.
- ❑ The playground area (ground surface and equipment) is in safe condition.
- ❑ The fences/walls lining the area are in good repair.
- ❑ Sidewalks are without cracks, separations, or raised concrete.

Equipment

- ❑ Nets are in good shape.
- ❑ Tennis balls are available for practice and match play.

Other

- ❑ Drinking water is readily available.
- ❑ A fully stocked first aid kit is available.

Informed Consent Form

I hereby give my permission for ________________________ to participate in ___________________________ during the athletic season beginning on ___________________________. Further, I authorize the school, league, or club to provide emergency treatment of any injury or illness my child may experience if qualified medical personnel consider treatment necessary and perform the treatment. This authorization is granted only if I cannot be reached and reasonable effort has been made to do so.

Parent or guardian: ____
Address: ____
Phone: (   ) ____________________ Other phone: (   ) ____________________

Additional contact: ____
Relationship to athlete: ______________________ Phone: (   ) ______________

Physician: ________________________________ Phone: (   ) ______________

Medical conditions (e.g., allergies, chronic illness): ______________________
____
____
____
____

My child and I are aware that participating in ____________________ is a potentially hazardous activity. We assume all risks associated with participation in this sport, including but not limited to: falls, contact with other participants, the effects of weather, traffic, and any other reasonable-risk conditions associated with the sport. All such risks to my child are known and appreciated by my child and me.

We understand this informed consent form and agree to its conditions.

Athlete signature: ____

Date: ___________

Parent or guardian signature: _____________________________________
Date: ___________

From ASEP, 2008, *Coaching youth tennis*, 4th ed. (Champaign, IL: Human Kinetics).

Injury Report Form

Date of injury: ______________________ Time: _______________ a.m./p.m.
Location: ____

Athlete name: ____
Age: ____________ Date of birth: ________________________________

Type of injury: ____
Anatomical area involved: _______________________________________
Cause of injury: ____
____
____
____

Extent of injury: ____
____
____
____

Person administering first aid: ___________________________________
First aid given: ____
____
____

Other treatment given: ____
____
____

Referral action: ____
____
____
____
____

Signature of first-aid provider: ___________________________________
Date: ____________

Emergency Information Card

Athlete name: ______________________________ Date of birth: ____________
Address: ____
Phone: (   ) _________________________

Contact Information

Parent or guardian: ____
Address: ____
Phone: (   ) ____________________ Other phone: (   ) ____________________

Additional contact: ____
Relationship to athlete: ____
Address: ____
Phone: (   ) ____________________ Other phone: (   ) ____________________

Insurance Information

Insurance company: ____
Address: ____
Named insured: __________________ Policy number: ____________________

Medical Information

Physician: ____
Address: ____
Phone: (   ) _________________________

Is your child allergic to any drugs? *YES* *NO*
If yes, please list ____
Does your child have other allergies (e.g., bee stings, dust)? *YES* *NO*
If yes, please list ____
Does your child have any of the following? *asthma* *diabetes* *epilepsy*
If yes, please list any special needs ______________________________
Is your child currently taking medication? *YES* *NO*
If yes, please list ____
Does your child wear either of the following? *glasses* *contact lenses*
Are there any other concerns about your child's health? *YES* *NO*
If yes, please list: ____

____

Parent or guardian signature: ____
Date: ____________________

From ASEP, 2008, *Coaching youth tennis*, 4th ed. (Champaign, IL: Human Kinetics).

Emergency Response Card

Be prepared to give the following information to an EMS dispatcher. (*Note*: Do not hang up first. Let the EMS dispatcher hang up first.)

Name: ____

Number dialing from: (   ) ______________________________

Reason for call: __________________________________

Number of people injured: __________________________

Condition of injured: _____________________________

First aid being given: _____________________________

____

Current location: _________________________________

Address: ____

City: ____

Directions (please note cross streets, landmarks, entrance access, etc.):

From ASEP, 2008, *Coaching youth tennis*, 4th ed. (Champaign, IL: Human Kinetics).

Appendix B

Tennis Terms

ace—A ball that is served so well that the opponent cannot touch it.

ad (short for advantage)—The point scored after deuce. If the serving side scores, it is ad-in; if the receiving side scores, it is ad-out.

ad court—The returner's left court. All odd-numbered points are played in the ad court. All points after deuce, either ad-in or ad-out, are played in the ad court.

all—An even score (30-all, 3-all, etc.).

alley—The area between the singles and doubles sidelines on each side of the court. (The singles court is made wider for doubles by the addition of the alley.)

approach—A shot, hit just before a player comes to the net, that puts the opponent on the defensive.

backcourt—The area between the service line and the baseline.

backhand—The stroke used to return balls hit to the left side of a right-handed player and to the right side of a left-handed player.

backspin—The backward rotation of the ball caused by hitting high to level under the ball. This is also called underspin.

baseline—The end lines of the tennis court that are parallel to the net.

center mark—The small line extending 4 inches into the court from the center of the baseline.

center service line—The line that divides the service courts into the deuce court and the ad court. The line is perpendicular to the net in the center of the court extending from the net to the service line on both sides of the court.

choke up—To grip the racket up toward the head.

crosscourt shot—A ball hit diagonally across the court.

deep serve—A serve that bounces in the service court near the service line.

deep shot—A shot that bounces in play near the baseline.

deuce—A score of 40-40 (the score is tied and each side has won at least 3 points).

deuce court—The right court, so called because on a deuce score the ball is served there. All even-numbered points are played in the deuce court.

double fault—The failure of both service attempts; the server loses the point.

doubles—A match with four players, two on each team.

doubles sideline—Lines set wider than singles sidelines, making the court wider for doubles play.

down-the-line shot—A ball that follows closely the path of a sideline.

drop shot—A ball falling quickly into the forecourt after crossing the net.

fault—A serve that lands outside the service court.

flat shot (flat serve)—A shot that travels in a straight line with little arc and little spin.

foot fault—A fault called against the server for stepping on the baseline or into the court with either foot during the serve.

forecourt—The area between the service line and the net.

forehand—The stroke used to return balls hit to the right of a right-handed player and to the left of a left-handed player.

game—A series of points. A game comprises a predetermined number of points and varies by age group.

good ball—A ball in play that lands in the court (or on any part of a line forming the boundary of the court).

ground stroke—A stroke, forehand or backhand, made after the ball has bounced.

half-volley—A stroke made by hitting a ball immediately after it has touched the ground.

let—A point played over because of interference. Also, a serve that hits the top of the net but is otherwise good, in which case the serve is taken again.

lob—A ground stroke that lifts the ball high in the air, usually over the head of the net player.

lob volley—A volley stroke hit over the head of the opponent.

love—Zero (no score).

match—Either two out of three games or two out of three sets, depending on the age group.

net game—Play in the forecourt close to the net.

out—A ball landing outside the boundary lines of the court.

overhead—A stroke made with the racket above the head.

poach—To hit a ball in doubles, usually at the net, that normally would have been played by one's partner.

point—The smallest unit of scoring. A point begins with the serve and goes until one player cannot return the ball over the net and in the court.

rally—A series of good hits made successively. Also, the practice procedure in which players hit back and forth to each other.

receiver—The player who receives the service.

serve (short for service)—The act of putting the ball into play for each point.

server—The player who serves.

service boxes—The court where serves must land.

service break—A game won by the opponent of the server.

service line—The line that runs parallel to the net from sideline to sideline.

set—A series of games, the number of which varies by age group.

shot—The hitting of the ball across the net and into the court on the other side.

singles—A match between two players.

singles sideline—Lines that run perpendicular to the net from baseline to baseline to form the singles court.

slice—To hit a ball with sidespin, like the spin of a top.

smash—A hard overhead shot.

spin—The rotation of the ball.

stroke—The act of striking the ball with the racket.

tiebreak—A system used to decide a set when the score is tied either at four-all for players 10 and under or six-all for players 12 and over.

topspin—The forward rotation of the ball caused by brushing from low to high behind the ball.

volley—A stroke made by hitting a ball before it has touched the ground.

Appendix C

21 Tennis Activities

The 21 activities found here differ from the technique drills in chapter 7 because they focus on creating matchlike scenarios, distinguishing teams, and setting up scoring situations. As a youth tennis coach, you will want to use the technique drills in chapter 7 to help your players progress in skill level and the matchlike activities described here to keep motivation high and make the sport fun.

As you're setting up your practices and using matchlike activities, keep in mind that these activities

- can handle four to eight players per court,
- can be conducted by the coach or the players themselves,
- are adaptable to various skill levels, and
- teach both technical and tactical issues.

Alley Rally

Objective

To develop steadiness and accuracy on ground strokes

Description

Players work in pairs, stationed on opposite ends of the court. One puts the ball into play using a drop hit, and the players begin a rally. All shots must land in the alley to be good. After an error, the player who initially put the ball into play begins the next point, until he has begun play five times. The other player then initiates the next 5 points, and the game continues until one player reaches 21 points.

Variations

- Begin players at the service lines and use foam balls so they will have time to set up and hit their most accurate shots.
- Use a shorter court and low-compression balls.
- Stretch a rope across the net at a height of 6 feet to help players aim higher for more depth and safety.

All Position Doubles

Objective

To play points from all positions on the court and to keep players moving

Description

Split players into four groups. The first player in each group takes a doubles position on the court and plays a point that can begin with a drop hit or serve. Once the point is played, the next player in each group rotates in and takes a position on the court, while the original player takes a position at the end of another group's line. After the rotation, another point is played. After the point is over, players rotate again, as described previously.

Attack Serve and Take Net

Objective

To hit a deep approach shot and take the net

Description

Players play singles or doubles. The serving team is allowed only one serve and may not follow it to the net. The receiver should drive the ball deep and move into a net position to attack. Players play the point out and keep regular score.

Variation

- After a period of time, have the receiver vary returns by hitting them short to force the server to move forward to lift the ball.

Baseline Doubles

Objective

To practice the transition to the net from the baseline

Description

Two teams of two players each begin at the baseline. One team puts the ball in play with a drop hit, and a rally begins. When one player gets a short ball that lands inside the service line, she must move in to play an approach shot, and her partner moves in also. Play continues, with the defending team using drives and lobs while the net players try to put the ball away. Play continues to 5 points, at which point teams switch to begin the next 5 points. Fifteen points wins the game.

Beat Mr. Nobody

Objective

To develop serve consistency

Description

Players serve a complete game against an imaginary opponent. As long as the serve goes into the proper box, the player wins the point. Mr. Nobody wins a point only on a double fault. To accommodate more than one player at a time, have players rotate in to serve their first point. Players serve the number of complete games that time allows. This is a good activity for players to accomplish alone with a basket of balls outside of team practice or in case of an injury that prevents running.

Variation

- As players gain control of direction, require the serve to land in either the outside or inside half of the proper service box. This reduces the size of the target and requires greater directional control.

Champs and Chumps

Objective

To develop singles tactics in match conditions with multiple players on one court

Description

Using a minimum of six players, line players up behind the baseline on each side of the court. One side of the court is designated as the champions' side; the other side is called the chumps' side. The first player from each side plays out a point (the ball is put into play by the player on the champions' side) using singles court boundaries. The player who wins the point goes to the end of the champions' line, whereas the loser goes to the end of the chumps' line. The other players rotate through their lines in order. Players can start the point with a drop hit from the baseline or a serve.

Champion of the Court

Objective

To develop singles tactics

Description

A designated champion competes against a line of at least three challengers. The champion assumes a baseline position on one side of the court. Other players (i.e., the challengers) wait at the back of the opposite side of the court. The first challenger assumes an opposite baseline position and drop hits or serves the ball to the champion. A point is played using the singles court boundaries. If the challenger wins, he is the new champion and runs to the other side of the court (to the champion's side). If the champion wins, she stays and plays a point against the next challenger.

Variations

- Require that the challengers win 3 points before becoming the champion.
- Play as doubles, using two champions against two challengers.

Circle Volley

Objective

To improve volley consistency with a group

Description

Players stand in a circle with their rackets in a volley ready position. One player hits a foam ball toward another player. That player must volley the ball to another player around the circle. Players cannot play two shots in a row. Players in the circle should count how many volleys they can hit in a row before the ball bounces.

Variation

- As the players improve, enlarge the circle or replace the foam ball with a low-compression ball or a regulation ball.

One Ball Live

Objective

To develop consistency with ground strokes and transitions into either offensive or defensive doubles situations

Description

Using a minimum of four players, have two sets of players rally with one another in a "split court" setup, in which the court is halved vertically. Two balls are put into play with a drop hit for two simultaneous rallies. Once an error is made, the player making the error calls out "one ball live!" and the remaining ball is played out among the four players. The winning team scores a point and stays to play against two new players. Teams continue to rotate until one of them reaches 10 points and is declared the winner.

Variation

- The court can be split diagonally so that the game is played crosscourt.

Shadow Doubles

Objective

To play doubles points with serves and volleys

Description

The game is played like doubles and as though there are four players, but only two players are on the court. One side is designated the serving side, and the other is the receiving side. The server puts the ball into play by serving and can return the ball using only a volley. All shots must be hit crosscourt into the area between the center line and the doubles sideline. The point is played until conclusion, at which point the players switch roles. Play continues until one player has reached 5 points.

Variations

- Require the receiver to hit specific strokes.
- Allow the server only one serve.

Stop Sign Volley Tap

Objective

To introduce volley skills

Description

Players work in pairs, standing no more than 5 feet apart. One player tosses the ball underhanded to the partner. The hitter holds the racket to the forehand side as if signaling "Stop!" The hitter gently taps the ball back to the feeder, who catches it, and the sequence is repeated five times before players switch roles.

Variations

- Have players use a backhand volley.
- Require that players use only one hand.
- Add competition between teams to see who can be the first to successfully complete 20 volleys and catches.

Tag Team Singles

Objective

To develop singles tactics and awareness of court positioning

Description

Using a minimum of four players, split players into two teams. Each team forms a line behind the middle of each baseline with one player at the baseline on each side. One player drop hits the ball and runs to the back of his line. The player at the front of the line on the other team returns the ball and runs to the back of his line. The teams keep the point going until one team misses. Each team keeps track of its points. The first team to 10 points is declared the winner.

Variations

- A team loses a point if a player hits the ball inside the service line.
- Give each team only one racket.

Team Doubles

Objective

To learn to play doubles points from all four positions

Description

Four players assume the typical doubles positions on each side of the court. One side is the serving side and one side is the returning side. Points can begin with a drop hit, serve, or feed from the coach. After a point is played, players take turns rotating one spot on their side of the net. Games can be played to a predetermined number of points with teams switching sides of the court after each game. One team serves the entire game, and all serves are from the deuce court.

Variations

- Allow only one serve, to have players work on consistency.
- Award two points for a winning volley.
- Require returns to be lobs.
- Require that the server follow the serve to the net.

The Deep Game

Objective

To test players' ability to keep ground strokes deep in the court

Description

Two players are at opposite baselines. One player begins the point with a drop hit. Each player earns 1 point every time the ball lands in the court and 2 points when the ball lands on or behind the service line. Players must call out their scores each time they score a point. The goal is to see which player reaches 21 points first. After one game, players change ends, and the other player begins the points with a drop hit.

Variations

- Use only half the court (divide the court down the middle) so four players can be on one court.
- Have players begin play with a serve and return. The server just tries for steadiness, whereas the receiver must hit all balls deep.
- As skill level increases, require that deep shots land at three-quarters court or beyond to count.

Three-Shot Tennis

Objective

To develop consistency in beginning a point

Description

Two players begin a singles point with the serve, the return, and the first ground stroke. All three shots must be successful or the players must begin the point again. If the three shots are good, play continues until one player wins the point. Use normal scoring. The goal is to impress players with the importance of getting the first shots of a point into play.

Variation

- To increase the difficulty, allow only one serve and require the service return to land beyond the service line.

Triples

Objective

To develop quick reactions at the net and accuracy and consistency from the baseline

Description

Divide players into two teams of three to six players each. Each team forms a triangle on each side of the net with one person at the net and two players behind the baseline. Extra players wait at the back fence to fill in from the baseline after each point. The game is started by a player at the baseline who drop hits a ground stroke. Using the entire doubles court, points are played three against three encouraging the net player to move and intercept as many balls as possible to play a volley. After each point, players rotate clockwise, with an extra player entering, if applicable. The first team to win 10 points wins the game.

Variation

- When a player is not in position or off balance at the baseline, do not allow lobs, which will give the net player an opportunity to volley a weak return.

Two Points at the Net

Objective

To encourage players to seize the net

Description

Use normal scoring but award two points when the winning shot is hit at the net on a volley or smash. The next point is then played from the same side of the court to keep the score and side in proper rotation.

Variation

- Add bonus points for any strategic move that you want to emphasize and reward, such as lobbing to take the net or hitting a winning shot down the middle.

About ASEP and the USTA

Coaching Youth Tennis was written by the American Sport Education Program (ASEP) in conjunction with the United States Tennis Association (USTA). ASEP has been developing and delivering coaching education courses since 1981. As the nation's leading coaching education program, ASEP works with national, state, and local youth sport organizations to develop educational programs for coaches, officials, administrators, and parents. These programs incorporate ASEP's philosophy of "Athletes first, winning second."

The USTA is the national governing body for the sport of tennis and the recognized leader in promoting and developing the sport's growth on every level in the United States, from local communities to the crown jewel of the professional game, the US Open. Established in 1881, the USTA is a progressive and diverse not-for-profit organization whose volunteers, professional staff, and financial resources support a single mission: to promote and develop the growth of tennis. The USTA is the largest tennis organization in the world, with 17 geographical sections, more than 700,000 individual members and 7,000 organizational members, thousands of volunteers, and a professional staff dedicated to growing the game.

USTA Jr. Team Tennis is the largest youth tennis league in the country, helping girls and boys ages 6 to 18 get in the game, get on the court, and have a good time. Teams are coed and made up of at least six players (three boys and three girls) based on similar ages and skill levels. The emphasis is on skill development, fun, teamwork, and friendly competition, all with the possibility of advancing to the national championship. Tennis is a sport individuals can play for life, and Jr. Team Tennis lays the foundation for a lasting relationship.